GHOSTS AND LEGENDS OF ALCATRAZ

GHOSTS AND LEGENDS OF ALCATRAZ

BOB DAVIS AND BRIAN CLUNE

FOREWORD BY JANICE OBERDING

Haunted America

The iconic Alcatraz guard tower overlooking San Francisco Bay and the city skyline.

Published by Haunted America
A Division of The History Press
Charleston, SC
www.historypress.com

All images are from the authors' collection unless otherwise noted.

First published 2019

Manufactured in the United States

ISBN 9781467143875

Library of Congress Control Number: 2019943363

Ash and Laurel Blackwell were with us that first night we spent on Alcatraz. Ash had one of the most terrifying events any of us have had happen to us while investigating the medical isolation ward, and none of us shall ever forget what occurred…or him. For that, we dedicate this book to him and Laurel. They are both family and always will be.

This modern welcome greets visitors when first arriving on Alcatraz.

The public never wanted to know the real Alcatraz. Even today, after the prison has been closed for so many decades, the public just won't let go of the myths.

—Philip Bergan, former captain of the guards

CONTENTS

FOREWORD

Ask anyone who's ever visited Alcatraz; there's no question that it is haunted. In fact, many people consider it to be one of the most haunted places in the United States. You only have to look at both the island's and the former federal prison's history to find good reason for this. Is it any wonder that there are a number of books about Alcatraz? That said, *Ghosts and Legends of Alcatraz* is my favorite. There are two reasons for this: it was written by my friends Brian Clune and Bob Davis, and it's a damn good book.

Historians/paranormal research investigators Brian Clune and Bob Davis are two of only a very few writers who could have tackled a book such as *Ghosts and Legends of Alcatraz*. After just a few pages, you'll realize that this is not an Alcatraz fluff piece but a thoroughly researched book. Many writers cover history very well. Many writers cover the paranormal very well. Brian and Bob are the rare writers who do both. They skillfully blend the historic with the paranormal aspects of Alcatraz so that one does not overshadow the other. And as a writer, I can tell you that this is no easy task.

As an avid reader of regional ghost/history books, I have read Brian and Bob's other books, *Ghosts of the Queen Mary*, *Haunted San Pedro* and *Haunted Universal Studios*. In *Ghosts and Legends of Alcatraz*, they again write a book that incorporates the three important components that readers want in a book: it should be informative, accurate and entertaining.

There are no delusions regarding the cons who called Alcatraz home. Brian and Bob set the record straight. In the 1962 film *The Birdman of Alcatraz*, actor Burt Lancaster's portrayal of the Birdman, Robert Stroud, garners sympathy for the kindhearted amateur ornithologist. Nice, but not true. *Ghosts and Legends of Alcatraz* will enlighten you on the real Robert Stroud, who was nothing like Lancaster's character. Admittedly, the Birdman always seemed rather creepy to me, and I was surprised to learn that he had written two books while in Alcatraz. Both books were published posthumously. For some writers, that might be just as well. Having not read Stroud's books, I cannot say if this is the case. I can say that while Brian and Bob tell of Stroud's, Al Capone's and Alvin "Creepy" Karpis's haunting their old stomping grounds, they admirably step away from trying to answer the old question, *Why would someone haunt a place they hated?* They eloquently state, *I don't know.* And what can be more honest than that?

While sharing the ghostly experiences of others, Brian and Bob do not try to analyze those experiences. They present the stories without obtrusively categorizing the ghosts and hauntings as they go along. I like that in a book, and I bet I am not alone in this regard. Tell me the stories; spare me the paranormal psychoanalysis. With apologies, I borrow from the Bard and will ask, what's in a name? That which we call a ghost by any other name would haunt as effectively.

When I read a book about history/hauntings, I don't want to read pretentious hair-splitting categorizing of the ghost in residence. I want to read about the *ghosts*. How do they appear? What are they doing, saying or not? Inform me, entertain me and be accurate while doing so. In *Ghosts and Legends of Alcatraz*, Brian and Bob do. I know this because I, too, have visited Alcatraz overnight and experienced its ghosts.

The first time I saw Alcatraz, I was a child, and it was still very much a federal prison. My family and I were on one of the Red and White Fleet boats that skirted the island, careful to keep the legal distance, lest any athletic inmate swim out and commandeer our boat. Of course, that wasn't going to happen. But I allowed myself to believe it possible. Because after all, I knew some very bad men were housed there. I didn't watch Eliot Ness and all those other crime fighters on the family's twenty-one-inch black-and-white Zenith for nothing.

It would be several years before I was able to actually spend the night on Alcatraz, and it was a streak of luck that put me there. At that time, there was something like a raffle system, and groups could put their name in the hat. Only so many were drawn. If you were the lucky winner, you paid about $1,500 to spend the night on the island with your group. The date you were to do so was written in stone. If you couldn't or wouldn't take your assigned date, you lost out. I was fortunate that a friend won and invited me, Mark and Debby Constantino, Patrick Burns and a group of San Francisco ghost hunters to spend the night. I traveled down to San Francisco with Mark and Debby and was ready for a great investigation. And there I was, in Al Capone's cell, calling to the old crime boss to speak into my recorder. He didn't. Neither did the Birdman or any other con. I didn't blame them too much. I was here of my own free will, and they were there through no choice of their own. Unlike the cons, I could walk up to the building assigned for a snack anytime I wanted. Standing on the old worn-out linoleum floor of the cafeteria, I thought of the food served here and the men who either ate it or went hungry. This was not a posh place of penitence. This was a place of punishment. If you did the crime, you were going to do the time. And it wasn't going to be pleasantly spent but rather in a cell no bigger than most people's linen closet.

As the night wore on, Alcatraz grew colder and colder until our teeth chattered. Wrapped up in coats and blankets we'd been smart enough to bring, we continued our exploration of Alcatraz, aka the Rock. We were here and we weren't going anywhere until the boatload of tourists arrived in the morning. Many people in our group of about twenty-five had ghostly experiences. A woman received an EVP (electronic voice phenomenon) that contained a string of four-letter words when she asked, "If you're here, will you please speak to me?" Needless to say, she didn't ask that question again.

During the night, one man encountered a child's ghost. We believe that to be one of the children who lived here on the island while their dads kept the inmates in line. The one memory I especially treasure is of a recording in the hospital surgery wing with Mark and Debby. Just us and two other people, we walked around the room gathering our thoughts. Debby felt that the ghost was an inmate. I felt that he was a guilt-ridden alcoholic doctor whose patient had died. So we turned on our recorders and asked the old question, "Do you have anything to tell us?"

"Dr. Thompson here and I'm ready to travel," came the reply.

To us, that was amazing, and we were glad to get the EVP—just as long as the good doctor traveled with someone else. The last thing anyone wants is a ghost who follows them home.

I returned to Alcatraz a few years later with the Ghost Hunters, Jason Hawes and Grant Wilson, for a TV shoot. Both men were very charming and kind. Alcatraz was still haunted. And as the fog rolled in off San Francisco Bay, it was still cold and damp enough to wish for a warm blanket and a cup of chicken noodle soup. Neither was forthcoming. Alas, my brilliant monologue ended up on the cutting room floor. But it's all good. The view of San Francisco's city lights across the bay from Alcatraz is phenomenal. The ghosts on Alcatraz are truly amazing—and real.

I only wish that Brian and Bob's book *Ghosts and Legends of Alcatraz* had been available when I first visited Alcatraz. I just know you'll want to read this book and keep it handy as a reference when next you visit Alcatraz, or, as Brian and Bob call it, "Hellcatraz!"

—Janice Oberding,
author of *Haunted Virginia City*, *Haunted Reno* and *Haunted Lake Tahoe*.
Janice has also appeared on numerous paranormal TV shows.

ACKNOWLEDGEMENTS

A s always, we would like to thank our ever-patient editor, Laurie Krill. We think she had to put up with more questions with this book than any other. We would also like to thank all of those who told us their stories for inclusion in the book, especially those rangers and employees of Alcatraz. Thank you for the trust you put in us.

We would also like to thank our readers. Without you, there would be no reason to continue to write. Of course, we must thank our families, who again had to put up with many hours of research and writing that take away from our time at home. We will forever be grateful.

Most of all, we would like to thank Delia Summerfield for her years of working on our websites, having to field all of our non-techie questions and having to deal with our radio clients, all while trying to raise her beautiful family. You will always be a part of our family, Delia, and a member of Planet Paranormal.

The Alcatraz water tower still holds the scars of the Indian occupation.

Introduction to America's Devil's Island

lcatraz Island, the Rock—the name alone conjures up images of Al Capone, Robert Stroud (the Birdman) and, of course, the famed *Escape from Alcatraz*. This small rocky outcropping in the middle of San Francisco Bay has achieved fame worldwide and has become the number-one tourist destination in San Francisco and one of the most visited spots in all of the United States.

How did a barren rock populated by birds become such a famous location throughout the world? What is it about this tiny outcropping that has captured the imagination of people everywhere from Asia to Europe? Is it the Ohlone history that people flock to see? Maybe it is the allure of the American gangster that draws in those who long for the simpler times of the Roaring Twenties, when the economic outlook was bright, Art Deco was in vogue and flappers danced the night away to jazz music. A time when Prohibition turned criminals into blue-collar heroes running whiskey, moonshine and hooch to underground speakeasies where the rich and poor would mingle as equals for the pleasure of illicit booze. When the likes of "Machine Gun" Kelly, Al "Scarface" Capone and public enemy no. 1 Alvin Karpis walked the halls of the most famous lockup but were considered folk heroes among the poor and destitute in the dust bowls and shanty towns of the Great Depression.

Perhaps the draw of Alcatraz goes deeper into the human psyche, to that place few like to think about. To a corner of the mind that both lures the imagination while at the same time repels rational thought and the ideas that the imagination brings forth. A place where nightmares hide and insanity edges to the surface. A place we all know exists while our beliefs tell us it can't actually be true. Some call it legend, others call it mystical, but we know what it truly is: the spirits of the past haunting the place that gave them torment and pain. For Alcatraz is one of the most haunted places on Earth.

Alcatraz was a prison, a military post and a place of both refuge and exile. It has changed the lives of countless people over its existence, from the time of the Native American tribes to the convicts who called the island home—and it is still changing the lives of tourists and others today.

The number of visitors to the prison reporting paranormal activity hasn't declined since the day it opened as a tourist attraction; on the contrary, it seems the reports have only grown. For many of the tourists visiting Alcatraz, the experience has not only given them something to tell their grandchildren, but for a few, it has actually changed their lives. Such was the case for co-author Bob Davis when he and his family spent the day on Alcatraz when Bob was just a young boy.

Bob Davis and his family touring Alcatraz moments before his life was forever changed.

In the spring of 1973, Planet Paranormal founder Bob Davis went to Alcatraz with his family for a day of sightseeing and exploration of the famous prison. While on the tour of the jail cells, they came to infamous D Block and its five solitary confinement cells. At that time, the doors could still be shut, and it was common practice for the guides to ask for volunteers to be "locked" into the most nefarious of them all, 14D. Bob, being a thirteen-year-old non-believer in ghosts, readily raised his hand to be the one placed in the tiny cell. He was the only one, in fact, to volunteer.

As the steel door slammed shut, Bob was plunged into total darkness. This didn't bother him, but he was keenly aware of the cramped quarters he found himself in. As he stood there in the blackness, he heard the tour guide call out from the other side of the door asking if he was all right, and Bob immediately called back that he was fine. That's when he felt a strong hand grip his shoulder and heard a voice whisper directly into his ear. In a menacing, evil tone and with a tightening of the grip on the boy's shoulder, a man said, "You're mine."

Bob began to pound on the door of the cell and frantically asked to be let out. From that day forward, Bob has been on a quest to discover the mysteries of the paranormal world. Bob likes to joke about the fact that he "went into that cell as an atheist and came out a Christian."

This is but one small way the island has forever changed the lives of those who venture onto its shores. For a small boy, those changes can be so dramatic as to send him on a lifelong search for answers into what he experienced that day.

Tourists are not the only ones who have had their lives upended by the strange and unusual things that happen on Alcatraz. Tour guides and the National Park rangers have had countless experiences while working and spending the night guarding the island. Unfortunately, the National Park Service has a standing gag order prohibiting employees from talking about the paranormal occurring on Alcatraz, but as fortune would have it, over the many years we have been investigating the island, we have found a few to tell us some of the incredible things that have happened to them and their colleagues while tending to their duties. These employees have asked us, at the risk of termination, to please not mention their names, and we will never dishonor that trust. Hopefully, one day the federal government will allow an open and free discussion of this island to be brought forth.

Whatever one must think about Alcatraz and its ghosts and legends, one thing is clear from the history of this amazing region: Alcatraz stands out among all of the odd and bizarre stories that have come from this progressive

The morgue on the island, where many prisoners found themselves after failed escape attempts.

and socially diverse city on the bay and is just one more reason why San Francisco is known around the world as a hotbed of paranormal activity.

With the tales of attempted escapes and its violent past as a prison, its time as a military citadel with all of the inherent dangers that brings and the Ohlone tribe's use of the island as a place of exile, coupled with the legends of evil beasts and deadly spirits of folklore, is it any wonder that this tiny speck of rock in the middle of a dangerous, roiling bay would come to be known as America's Devil's Island?

CHAPTER 1
THE OHLONE AND THE EVIL SPIRITS

L ong before the waters of the Pacific Ocean filled the basin we now
know as San Francisco Bay, the Ohlone tribes called the area around
Alcatraz home. Then, Angel Island as well as Alcatraz were mountain
peaks that were hunted by the tribes and their trees used for firewood.
When the Pacific claimed the lower sections, the Ohlone simply moved and
continued life in what is now the Bay Area.

The Ohlone tribes lived in relative peace with each other, although they
were territorial and would war with one another from time to time. They
worshipped the spirits of the plants, the animals and mother earth. To
them, life was a cycle of birth, death and rebirth, a great circle of life that
was interdependent on all living things. As an Ohlone explained it, "We
die, the grass grows, the rabbit eats the grass, the birds eat the rabbit and
then we become a part of everything; the trees, bushes, rabbits and birds,
even the ocean itself."

The Ohlone lived in communal villages, and all of the people were
considered equal within the tribe. They did have a chief, usually an elder, but
he generally was considered more of an advisor, someone who only wielded
real authority among the people during times of war. The one in the tribe
who commanded the most respect and who was the most formidable figure
within the tribe was the shaman.

The shaman was thought to have supernatural powers brought on through
an ordeal or test he went through at an early age. Each shaman trained the
next in line, imparting unto the novice the powers and magics that would

The various officers' quarters have been said to be haunted, although no one has been allowed to officially investigate.

sustain and keep the tribe safe from evil spirits and their enemies. The shaman was highly respected for his abilities to heal the sick and perform the tribal rites. He was also the one person in the tribe who was almost universally feared.

For all of the equality within the tribe, individual freedoms were not the norm. The family unit was the most important aspect of tribal life for the Ohlone. Everything that was done by the head of the family was done for the family, never for the individual within the family. "A man is nothing, without his family he is less than a bug crossing the trail." This way of thinking was the cornerstone to the strength for all of the Ohlone tribes.

Life among the people was the same as for any other tribe throughout the Americas. The women would gather acorns and crush them into flour, then sift it through a finely woven basket. The flour would then be made into bread, mush and meal and eaten as the main staple for the tribe. The men would hunt, collect shellfish and fish the local waters. Even if the hunting and fishing were sparse, the women always made enough flour to keep the people fed until meat was again brought in by the men of the tribe. This didn't happen often, as the Ohlone hunters were legendary for their skill in bringing down deer and other prey, even in the leanest of times. The Ohlone lived like this for thousands of years. They were born, lived, married and died within the tribes and their lands—that is, until the Spaniards arrived in the Bay Area. In the wake of European exploration, the Ohlone lifestyle would forever change.

The first Spanish ship to enter the bay was in 1775. After the ship made landfall, the Spaniards noticed a group of people approaching. Not knowing the locals, the Spaniards were on guard but didn't make any provocative moves. The newcomers found the Ohlone hospitable and kind. The Karkin tribe took them to their village and treated them to a feast. In all, the first encounter between the two peoples was a great success. It was on this trip that Lieutenant Ayala found a small, desolate island not far from the mainland. Ayala wrote: "I was looking over the island I called Angels' Island, the largest one in the harbor....I was inclined to go farther and look over another island and found it quite barren and rugged and with no shelter for a ship's boats. I named it Ysla de Alcatrazes because of the large number of pelicans that were there."

Once the Spanish settled in Alta (their name) California, Father Junipero Serra arrived in Monterey and began setting up his missions, seven in all, around the area. This mission system would be the end of the Ohlone way of life and for the Ohlone themselves. Edward Castillo, of the California Indian Education Center and a Native American, wrote about the mission system: "A scheme of world conquest devised by the Roman Catholic Church and the empire of Spain was supposed to only be a ten-year endeavor of which the natives were to become the beneficiaries. Instead it became almost seventy years of slavery, dehumanization and cultural genocide for the Ohlone and California native people alike."

Whatever the reader feels the truth may be, one thing we can't dismiss is the fact that after the Spanish arrived in the area, the Ohlone population began to rapidly decline. Newly introduced diseases, unsanitary living conditions at the missions where many were forced to live and the killing by Spanish soldiers of those Ohlone who would not voluntarily convert through baptism caused a steep and immediate decline in the population. Of the approximately ten thousand Ohlone living at the start of the mission system in the 1770s, by 1830, that number had dropped to fewer than two thousand.

The Ohlone had used Alcatraz for hundreds of years as a fishing base. They also used the island as a sort of prison for the undesirables within the tribe and those who had broken tribal law. The only way on or off Alcatraz was by boat, and so those deemed guilty of an offense would be taken to the island and marooned there. The Ohlone who would fish off the island would bring out needed supplies and water and then depart for their day of fishing. These fishermen would spend as little time as possible on Alcatraz for fear of the evil spirits they believed were there, as well as the ghosts of past ancestors who couldn't find their peace in death. They also believed that those imprisoned on the island and who had died there would come back to seek revenge for their banishment and untimely deaths.

Witchcraft was a large part of the Ohlone myths, and when a person was thought to have "poisoned" another, the shaman would be called in to judge and, if necessary, protect the people from the sorcerer or witch. If the "poison" was thought to be in the form of a curse, the shaman would need to counter it. "Poisoning" was thought to be a great selfish act. If the shaman determined that the curse was for personal gain, the sorcerer or witch would be exiled to Alcatraz to live out their days in solitude or with others who had been banished. If the shaman deemed the offending act to be of a truly evil nature then the offender would be put to death. The bodies of the offenders were buried in mounds on Alcatraz. Their spirits were sentenced to forever walk the earth alone. That is, unless they found kindred spirits.

The Ohlone believed that spirits that shared the same feelings of love, greed, hate and vengeance could find each other and become aligned. The spirits could walk side by side and attempt to influence the living. Those spirits that were filled with love would walk among their people spreading goodwill and hope, trying to make the lives of those they touched happy and fulfilling. Then there were the entities that were filled with so much hate and evil that they spent their afterlives in the pursuit of making people suffer and live in fear. These evil spirits wanted nothing more than revenge upon those still living, believing that they were the cause of their suffering and torment. These spirits were thought to be those of the people who had been cast out, exiled for offenses or put to death for egregious acts against their fellow tribesmen. These evil entities were said to walk the shores of Alcatraz. People used the island as a stop for fishing and a place of rest along the shore but would only venture farther than the waterline to bury those deemed unworthy of a funeral pyre or for rituals conducted by the shamans to help keep the evil away from the fishermen who plied the waters near the island.

Once the Spaniards arrived and began the conversion of the Ohlone to Christianity, many of the people resisted. Those who refused to submit to the padres were rounded up and forced to convert under strict, slave-like control. Many of the Ohlone, Chumash and other native tribes were forced to flee and hide from the Spanish and began calling the Europeans monsters. They believed that the missionaries were the embodiment of the evil spirits sent to test them. It is a testament to the extent of this fear of the Spanish that the Ohlone hid out on Alcatraz, building small villages inland, knowing the Europeans wouldn't look for them on an island they knew the people feared.

Although the mission system ended around 1834, the damage had been done. The Ohlone population had dwindled to the point of being almost nonexistent. The people who remained went to work at the nearby ranchos in the hopes that they would blend in and escape further exploitation and persecution. With the arrival of the new American settlers and the gold rush fever, the situation for the Ohlone didn't get any better; in fact, it became a permanent detriment. Once the United States purchased California as part of the Treaty of Guadalupe-Hidalgo, America made plans to convert Alcatraz into a military fort to aid in the protection of the bay. This spelled the end of the Native American occupation and ownership of the island.

Even though America took control and ownership of Alcatraz, Native Americans continued to live on the island. Unfortunately, they did so as prisoners of the United States. The largest group of natives to be interned on Alcatraz took place in January 1895 when nineteen Moqui Hopi Indians were sent to the disciplinary barracks. Natives would be sent to Alcatraz throughout the late 1800s and early 1900s. Once the federal prison was set up, incarceration of Native Americans was confined to the same reasons as any other convicted felons: they had to earn their way onto America's Devil's Island.

When the prison system shut Alcatraz down for good, the island sat empty, but not for long. Almost a year after the island closed, a group of Sioux tribesmen, led by Richard McKenzie, took over the island and demanded that it be used as a Native American cultural center and university. The occupation on March 9, 1964, only lasted for four hours before the U.S. Coast Guard removed the five men. Later that same day, another group of Native Americans, fourteen in all, made their way to Alcatraz and spent the night, and then, after claiming the island by right of discovery, they left. The theme of this occupation and the demands for a cultural center and university would resurface again at the end of the decade, and the call for native unity would reverberate around the country and the world.

On November 20, 1969, seventy-nine Native Americans landed on Alcatraz and claimed the island as Indian land. The Coast Guard tried but failed to remove the occupiers, and their leader, Richard Oakes, sent a message to the Department of Interior office in San Francisco that said,

After the Native American takeover of Alcatraz in the 1970s, they put up signs around the island claiming it as their property. *Courtesy of the U.S. National Park Service.*

"We invite the United States to acknowledge our claim. The choice lies with the leaders of the American government to use violence upon us as before to remove us from our Great Spirit's land or, to institute a real change in dealing with the American Indian. We do not fear your threat to charge us with crimes on our land. We and all other oppressed peoples would welcome spectacle of proof before the world of your title by genocide. Nevertheless, we seek peace."

The occupiers were made up of a diverse group of tribes from around the country, including students, activists, married couples and children. One of those kids was future Hollywood star Benjamin Bratt, along with his siblings.

By Thanksgiving Day, hundreds of supporters had made their way to Alcatraz, and in December, Native American activist John Trundell began airing a daily broadcast from the island. Jim Thorpe's daughter and Alcatraz occupier Grace Thorpe helped convince a number of A-list celebrities, including Jane Fonda, Marlon Brando and Anthony Quinn, to visit the island to lend their "star power" to the cause, and rock band Creedence Clearwater Revival donated $15,000 for a supply boat to be purchased. With all of the publicity and Hollywood stardom attached to the occupation, Alcatraz was again becoming known around the world.

Everything was running smoothly and according to plan until January 5, 1970. On that fateful day, Yvonne Oakes, daughter of de facto leader Richard Oakes, fell three stories from a stairwell and died. Unable to reconcile his daughter's death and telling his followers he no longer had the heart to carry on, Oakes left the island. Once Oakes left Alcatraz, the movement began to fall apart. Many of the young people left the movement to return to school, and others decided to leave with Oakes. Two competing groups began fighting to see which would become the new leadership. Then there were the people from the San Francisco hippie movement who arrived on the island with their drug addictions and alcoholism and thought that the movement and Alcatraz were their own personal protest and new home. It got so bad that the Native American occupiers prohibited all non-Indians from staying the night.

The federal government had adopted a hands-off approach to the occupation in the hopes that the occupiers would get bored or tired of the short rations they were forced to endure, but by mid-1970, those hopes were dwindling. To help speed things up, the feds decided to cut the electrical power to the island and removed the freshwater barge that they had brought out, which had provided drinking water for the occupiers. Three days after the barge was towed away, fires broke out on Alcatraz, which destroyed several of the historic buildings, including the warden's mansion, one of the most known and symbolic buildings on the island. The occupiers blamed the removal of the water barge for the fires and destruction and said that government infiltrators trying to turn away support for the movement had deliberately set the blazes. The feds blamed the occupiers for starting the fires in the buildings to keep warm and being negligent.

As the occupation continued into 1971, those on the island found their food and water supplies dwindling fast. In an effort to buy food, they began stripping Alcatraz of anything they could sell. They started ripping out any copper wiring and tubing they could find, along with other metals, and sold them as scrap. Three people were arrested and found guilty for theft of government property after selling six hundred pounds of copper. This, along with the fire and other destruction of property, caused the otherwise supportive press and media to turn on the occupiers. Stories emerged in the papers of alleged assaults and beatings, with one case being prosecuted in court. With the stories of abuse by and of the occupiers and reports of widespread destruction of the iconic and historic structures, support around the country and the world diminished to the point where none could be found.

When two oil tankers collided in the bay, even though it was determined that the unlit Alcatraz lighthouse wouldn't have prevented the mishap, the feds had finally had enough of the spectacle and destruction of the occupation. President Nixon gave the okay to have the Native Americans removed from the island as long as the use of force was kept to a minimum. Plans were drawn up to go in when the number of people on Alcatraz was at its smallest number so as to minimize confrontation. On June 10, 1971, FBI agents along with U.S. marshals and police officers took six unarmed men, five women and four children into custody and removed them from the island. The occupation of Alcatraz was over.

The Native Americans might not have achieved their goal of claiming ownership of Alcatraz, but their eighteen-month protest not only brought the plight of the United States' native population into focus on the world stage, it also awoke a new resolve to get the federal government to recognize the rights of the tribes to have self-determination and an end to the termination of tribes by Washington. Alcatraz might not have become part of the Nations, but Nixon returned forty-eight thousand acres of land in Blue Lake Pueblo to the Taos Indians, and land near Davis, California, became home to a Native American university. In Washington, D.C.,

Even today, the remnants of the Indian occupation are still present all over the island.

the Bureau of Indian Affairs began hiring Native Americans to work at the agency, and almost complete autonomy was granted to all Indian reservations and lands.

Along with the occupation of Alcatraz, more than two hundred instances of civil unrest among Native Americans occurred and brought further attention from around the world for what was happening to the indigenous population. With all that occurred within this relatively short time span, many scholars and historians credit the occupation as the "cradle of the modern Native American civil rights movement." And it may very well be. It does make one wonder, however, why the occupiers were so intent on making Alcatraz a symbol of the rebellion. After all, the island is essentially a barren, inhospitable rock unable to sustain life without aid. It might have something to do with an Ohlone legend of a creature fond of the Ohlone yet vengeful of those who harm them—a creature the Spanish had already met face to face.

CHAPTER 2

COLONIZATION AND THE RED-EYED BEAST

The first encounter between explorers and the native Californians didn't go too well. When the galleon *Nuestra Senora de Esperanza* made landfall at Morro Bay, it was met by hostile natives who killed some of the crewmen. Captain Pedro de Unamuno decided that further exploration was too dangerous and sailed off for safer ports. That didn't deter the Spanish from trekking ahead, and in the 1540s, Juan Rodríguez Cabrillo sailed as far north as present-day Oregon. Cabrillo made several landings along the way, and these went much better, with Cabrillo and his crew trading with the natives and building at least an amicable relationship. It would take another two hundred years before the Spanish gave serious consideration to claiming and colonizing Alta California.

Spain all but ignored California above its holdings in Baja and was content to have minor trading with the sometimes volatile native Californians. After the Seven Years' War changed the political landscape of Europe and with Russian fur traders working their way down from the Bering Sea, Spain believed that it was time to assert its control over what it saw as Spanish land. The expansion up the coast of California began in 1769 when the "Sacred Expedition" set sail, with another group on foot. These were led by Captain Gaspar de Portola and Franciscan missionary Father Junípero Serra. The first stop along the way was at San Diego, where a presidio (military fort) and mission church were erected. San Diego would become the first in a long line of settlements dominated by the Catholic Church and Spanish soldiers, who were the church's protectors and muscle.

By the end of the Spanish colonial period, presidios would be built at Santa Barbara, Monterey and at the harbor entrance in San Francisco. Each of these military forts was tasked not only with protecting the surrounding countryside from foreign incursions but also as a police force, if you will, to make sure that the missions were safe and that the Native Americans were kept in their place.

Spain used the mission system for hundreds of years as a way to colonize an area. Spain had always lacked a large number of settlers to colonize a new land, so it developed a system of using politics, economics and religious conversion of the native peoples as a way of Christianizing and Hispanicizing an area. The conquistadores would be the first into an area to pacify if necessary, followed by the padres, who would teach the natives the words of peace and sacrifice. The system had worked countless times over the years, but it was usually brought about by violence and slavery of the indigenous population.

The Franciscan friars were not a violent sect, and the missions were never meant to be harsh or overly destructive to native populations. The friars were, in fact, just overly pious to the point that they believed that whatever means they employed to bring the heathens to Christ were justified in their eyes. To this end, neophytes had to earn privileges through work, sacrifice and their knowledge of Christianity. Once brought into the mission system, the apprentices would not be allowed to venture outside the mission grounds until the priests deemed them "civilized" enough to spread the word of Christ and Spanish rule. To ensure that the natives toed the line, Spain made sure that each mission had a complement of Spanish soldiers on hand to deal with any neophyte or group who got out of hand. Effectively, the missions created a caste system. The priests were at the top, soldiers were in the middle and last came the Native American converts.

The three-tier system that the missions set up may have been good for the Spanish but not so much for the natives. The priests at the top of the ladder were treated more like royalty than the vow of poverty they had taken suggested. The soldiers, needing to be on the alert for trouble among the neophytes, didn't have to do much manual labor outside of cleaning their weapons and gear, which left the native people to do all of the menial labor. Farming, construction, food preparation, domicile and outbuilding cleaning and maintenance and any other work that needed to be done was undertaken by the native population. The Spanish, either by ignorance or intent, created a system of slavery that saw the native people providing for and waiting on their Spanish masters.

Over time, as is wont to happen, the Spanish, including the priests themselves, saw the natives as their servants rather than converts and began treating them as such, the soldiers going so far as to become hostile when they deemed the neophytes not behaving as the soldiers thought they should. The priests, on the other hand, still treated or tried to treat the natives with kindness, albeit a kindness tinged with contempt. This derision by a people they thought had their best interests in mind, along with the teachings of the priests that had little to do with how they were being treated, caused an almost complete disillusionment for the Ohlone and the other people who had not yet been brought into the mission system.

The native people began to hide away from the Spanish. They knew that if they were found, they would be forcibly removed from their lives and brought in for conversion to a faith that, to them, was duplicitous at best. Many people began working at the various ranchos around the area and used assumed names in an effort to disguise themselves. Others, not wanting to give in even that small amount, chose to hide on the surrounding islands of the bay. One of these was Alcatraz.

Even though the Ohlone knew that evil spirits might reside on the small rocky island, they felt it better to take their chances with the spirits rather than the Spaniards. The people also knew that the Spanish had their own superstitions about Alcatraz. The Spanish believed that a monster lived on the island and that not even the natives would dare to live alongside the red-eyed devil. The Ohlone, for their part, believed that the monster the Europeans were so afraid of was a creature sympathetic and kind to the native peoples of the area, the Matah Kagmi.

The Matah Kagmi is the Modoc name for Sasquatch, also known to Native Americans as Yah'yahaas, Chiye-Tanka or Maxemista. Whatever name one chooses to call the creature, most just call it Bigfoot. The legend of this creature goes back so far that no one can pinpoint exactly where the tales started. The one thing we do know is that the Native American culture is rife with stories of these beings that state that the creatures are not only intelligent but also sympathetic to the native people. Many stories tell of a lost, hurt or distressed native being helped or led to safety by one of these aloof creatures.

Perhaps the most famous of these took place in California in 1897. In that year, a Modoc man was walking down a deer trail after a day of fishing when he came upon a creature that was covered from head to foot by a thick, coarse hair. The creature gave off a strong musky odor, and the man realized he had come face to face with a Matah Kagmi. The man took a step closer,

As this photo shows, Alcatraz, as close as it is to the mainland, was still used by the Ohlone as a place to escape and to hide from their Spanish oppressors.

but a sound from the creature made the Modoc stop. It was growing dark, but the man could see through the thick hair of its head that the Matah Kagmi had soft brown eyes that seemed to hold no menace. The creature moved slightly in an inquisitive way, so the man, in a gesture of friendship, placed the string of fish he had been carrying in front of the creature and made a motion indicating the Matah Kagmi was welcome to them. The Matah Kagmi evidently understood, grabbed the fish and made its way back into the woods. As it disappeared from view, it stopped, turned back to the Modoc man and made a long, low sound like, "Aaagooomt." The man figured he would never see the creature again.

A few weeks after the encounter, the man was awakened one morning by a noise outside his cabin. When the man went to investigate, he found a stack of deer skin ready for tanning and heard the same sound he had heard when the creature turned to thank him for the fish. After this, from time to time the Modoc man would find other things left for him—berries, fruit, acorns and other things he might find himself in need of.

A few years later, the man was part of an expedition searching for gold in the area of Mount Shasta. At one point, the man was searching for gold when a rattlesnake bit him in the leg. The man killed the snake and headed back to camp but found that the bite and venom wouldn't allow him to make it back. The man found a comfortable spot to rest, figuring he would die in the mountains he loved. He got progressively sicker, even throwing up the contents of his stomach, and finally passed out from the wound.

The man awakened a few hours later and thought he must be dreaming. Around him stood three eight-to-ten-foot-tall Matah Kagmi. They had somehow managed to draw out some of the venom from the wound and placed a poultice of moss over the bite. One of the Matah Kagmi made a sound, and the other two picked up the man and began carrying him back down the trail. When they were close to the other members of the man's party, they carefully placed him under a bushy tree, made the sound that he had come to hear often when they left him gifts and walked back up the trail and out of sight.

The Modoc man never saw the creatures again, but for many years afterward, he would hear their call. The man said it was the "Matah Kagmi call." He would spend the rest of his life telling people who would listen that the Matah Kagmi were not the vicious beasts they were said to be. They were shy, aloof creatures, especially with the white man. They were mainly nocturnal and lived off of roots and berries and would only eat meat in the coldest winters when they couldn't find their normal foods. He also said that the Matah Kagmi could be fierce friends and even fiercer enemies. Those who treated their friends badly could expect retribution from the normally kind and peaceful creatures.

There are many within the Native American populace who believe that the Matah Kagmi, by whatever name they are called, are friends to the peoples. They believe that it could have been the Matah Kagmi that helped protect the Ohlone and other natives who sought refuge on the island of Alcatraz and the other islands. However, there are others who believe that it was something else, something that was not discriminate in its hatred for those still living. Those people believed that the evil that lived on the island of Alcatraz was the evil that the Ohlone originally feared and the reason they used Alcatraz as an island of exile and punishment: the Bukwus.

The Bukwus has been mistaken for Sasquatch so many times that people now believe they may be the same creature. Legend seems to dispute this in a number of different ways. The similarities are there only in one of the descriptions, that of both creatures being eight to ten feet tall and extremely hairy. This is where any comparison ends, however. Where the Matah Kagmi are seen as peaceful and to some extent benevolent, the Bukwus is the embodiment of evil.

According to legend, Bukwus are savage, human-like undead drowning victims. The Bukwus appear as zombie-like, hairy, bloated, decaying corpses. The Bukwus possess great physical strength and can become invisible to get close to their victims. These undead creatures are mostly found in forested areas near streams, lakes and rivers but are not limited to this. Because they are the tortured souls of those who have drowned and been turned into Bukwus by others who have gone before, they can be found anywhere there is a body of water where people can and have drowned. Many people have drowned around the rocky shores of Alcatraz since the first time people plied the waters of the bay looking for fish.

The Ohlone used Alcatraz as a place where they sent their condemned. They believed that the island was inhabited by evil spirits that would take the exiled, thereby punishing them for their transgressions. One of the traits of the Bukwus is that they try to take the living and turn them into Bukwus as well. The way the Bukwus did this was to offer the living a cockle shell filled with ghost food. If the living person was foolish enough to eat out of the shell, he or she would be turned into a Bukwus. Even if the person refused to eat the food, the Bukwus would attempt to drown their victim in an attempt to condemn him or her to an afterlife of eternal hunger, misery and wandering at the side of the Bukwus.

In some tales, the Bukwus would also feed on the corpses of small children they had lured into lakes and other water sources and drowned. This is not a widespread belief, but one tale that has been told many times is that when the Bukwus are ready for the kill, their eyes will glow a deep, bright red. This coincides with the legends that have sprung up on Alcatraz of a red-eyed monster that preys on the living. This tale has made its way from the early Ohlone tribes through the Spanish, Mexican and American occupations of the island and still persists to this day.

Considering what the Ohlone and other tribes of the area believed might lurk on Alcatraz, one must consider that they feared the Spanish soldiers and priests far more than the monsters they believed were living on the island. Alas, in the end it did them no good. The Spanish, wanting to make sure that their claim to the lands of California was theirs and theirs alone, hunted down most of the native peoples, including those hiding on Alcatraz.

When the Mexican government won its independence from Spain in 1822, the Native Americans were faced with a new set of challenges. The Mexicans were not interested in them as a source of slave labor, conversion or any other external need. The natives were simply ignored for the most part. After decades of hiding and being used and being taken care of, albeit

As the sun sets on one of Alcatraz's buildings, one can just imagine the many strange creatures the Ohlone and Spanish believed occupied the island.

savagely, they were now left to fend for themselves. The people did as they always had done and adapted.

The Mexican government put a low priority on San Francisco Bay, and as such, the defenses of the area fell into disrepair. The new commandant of the Presidio moved a large part of his garrison north to Sonoma, partly due to the deteriorating condition of the fort, and left the protection of the bay in the hands of only a few caretakers. Alcatraz was completely ignored and was never given a second thought.

In June 1846, American settlers, supported by a group of native Californians, revolted against the Mexican government of Alta California. Even though the Mexican-American War had already begun, the Mexicans were unprepared for what became known as the Bear Flag Revolt. The revolt was led by John C. Frémont and included mountain man Christopher "Kit" Carson. It didn't take Frémont's force long to reach the mouth of San Francisco Bay, and once there, he crossed the harbor at its narrowest point. When the Americans arrived at the lightly defended Presidio, the Mexican contingent fled, and Frémont and his men destroyed the cannons that were still there. Frémont declared California an independent republic and created a makeshift flag using a white bedsheet and, using red paint, placed a grizzly bear and lone red star on the sheet.

On July 9, 1846, Captain John Montgomery sailed the U.S. sloop *Portsmouth* into San Francisco Bay and landed a force of marines to seize the settlement of Yerba Buena, which later became known as the city of San Francisco. Two years later, the Treaty of Guadalupe-Hidalgo would end the conflict between Mexico and the United States. The American government would pay Mexico $15 million to establish the Rio Grande as the border between the two countries and grant the United States the areas now known as Texas, Nevada, Utah, Arizona, parts of Colorado, Wyoming and most of New Mexico. It also gave the United States complete control of California above Baja and agreed to assume all claims from private citizens against Mexico that were still pending.

The end of Spanish and Mexican rule over Alta California would bring many changes to the region and the San Francisco Bay. California would become a state of the United States in 1850, and no place would see bigger changes than the small island now officially known as Alcatraz.

CHAPTER 3

AMERICA AND THE MYSTERIOUS DRUMMERS

After the United States acquired Alta California, the government took control of the islands within San Francisco Bay. John Frémont would wage a one-man war against the United States for ownership of Alcatraz, but in the end, and after his court-martial, America became sole owner of the small rocky island. When gold was discovered at Sutter's Mill and trade increased as a result, the importance for defense of the San Francisco Bay increased with it. The government implemented a plan of coastal defense that would become known as the Plan of 1850.

The plan called for fortifications on both the north and south shores of the harbor entrance to catch incoming enemy ships in a crossfire, along with a third fortification inside the harbor on Alcatraz. This three-pronged attack would trap any ship in a deadly triangle of fire from the three forts, making any naval invasion unlikely to succeed. Construction of these forts would begin in 1853. Alcatraz would be the first completed by a good five years and would have the first permanent American guns, seven eight-inch and one ten-inch, placed on the Pacific coast.

When the American Civil War began, Washington realized that the Pacific coast was not only a prime target for the Confederacy but, as the British were reinforcing Vancouver Island, the threat of a British invasion of California while the United States was preoccupied became a very real concern. In response, the army built up Alcatraz with smaller and cheaper earthwork batteries that could house the new rifled cannons being installed at the other fortifications around the bay. These guns built up the firepower of Alcatraz to help combat the enemies' new ironclad ships that might try to enter the harbor. Along with the added fortifications, Alcatraz would also be used as a prison for deserters, malcontents and, as the war continued, Confederate prisoners of war.

The prison in use at this time was nothing more than a square cement holding tank underneath one of the sally ports of the guardhouse and was as sparse as a room could be. It was also often crowded with more prisoners than it could humanely house. It was cold and drafty, and many of those interred here came down with sicknesses and maladies that often went untreated and even killed the prisoners on occasion. At some time during the Civil War, a tuberculosis outbreak occurred in the prison "hole." As the inmates began to die and the disease spread, nurses from San Francisco volunteered to come to the island to treat the men who were locked up. Day and night these brave women tended to the victims. One of these nurses unfortunately contracted the disease, and army officials refused to allow her to leave the island. They wouldn't even allow her to leave the prison room. The nurse would die from her ailment, locked up and alone save for the criminals she had vowed to save. The disease was finally eradicated and the bodies removed to be buried in a mass quarantined grave, the brave nurse among the corpses. Today, the spirit of this nurse is still present in the room that was used as the prison and, as Planet Paranormal discovered, can also be found in the sally port directly above it.

As the Civil War came to a close, work once again commenced on building up the fortifications on Alcatraz. New funds were pumped into the island for upgrading the parapets, new magazines, platforms and higher brick walls. Military prisoners were often used to excavate rock and help with the construction. Armaments steadily increased on the island to a total of 155 guns, both mounted and unmounted. A new bombproof barracks and a pier were also built or started, along with a 180-foot-long tunnel through the island. This bore-cut tunnel is the genesis of the legend that Alcatraz is crisscrossed by secret tunnels. That same legend is still told today even though it has been consistently denied and proven false.

It was during this time that recommendations for the naming of Alcatraz's fort were put forth. The names were submitted to the general in command of the island and were those of officers from major up to general and also included commodores and admirals, all of whom had been killed in action during the Civil War, Mexican-American War or the Indian Wars. General Humphries chose James McPherson, an Alcatraz engineer who had been

The grate in the floor of this room leads to the original, now closed off prison once used by the military.

killed near Atlanta during the Civil War. Humphries forwarded the name to the secretary of war to rename Alcatraz Fort McPherson. The secretary ignored the recommendation, and Alcatraz has forever maintained the name that Lieutenant Ayala first gave the island.

One of the greatest changes to the island came about when a permanent quarters and parade grounds were required. The area chosen for this was on the southeast end of Alcatraz. This area, which still exists today, came about by the muscle and determination of the military prisoners who were tasked with the job. The plan called for this area to be cut down to sixty-two feet, which was accomplished using simple shovels and picks. All of the buildings are gone from this site today, but it is still visible from the many tour boats cruising past the island and from a vantage point near the lighthouse for those visiting Alcatraz.

Over the years since the end of the Civil War, the appropriations for Alcatraz had steadily dwindled. By 1877, Congress would fail to appropriate any funds at all. Alcatraz was not the only fort to suffer from lack of funds, but being on a non-self-sufficient island, it was hit particularly hard by the loss of any monies. When, in 1877–78, windstorms destroyed the wharf extensions constructed in 1867, the commanding general did not even propose replacing it. It became so bad that in April 1881, the commander put the island's steamer and scow up for sale. By 1884, even the crane servicing the wharf had been removed. The one bright spot during this period was when the Alcatraz quartermaster, who still had construction funds available, began work on remodeling the Citadel.

When the Spanish-American War broke out, it was expected that Alcatraz would receive funds to upgrade its armaments and once again take its place as the lynchpin of San Francisco Bay's defensive triangle. Unfortunately, that was not meant to be. Knowing that most of the guns placed on the island were woefully obsolete, it was decided that Alcatraz had no place in the defense of the bay. In 1900, the Ordnance Department began removing the obsolete smoothbore guns, sold their carriages and removed the two-hundred-pounder guns and also sold their mounts. By 1901, Alcatraz was completely void of coastal guns. Even though Alcatraz no longer had any defensive armament on the island, one thing was growing: the number of military prisoners.

It was about this time that stories of strange and disturbing things began to come to light on Alcatraz. While America had been busy building up the

A good example of the brick and mortar fortifications built throughout the island following the American Civil War.

island since the time it acquired it from Mexico, there were very few periods of inactivity on Alcatraz. With the hustle and bustle of all that had been going on, it's not surprising that the stories of the Ohlone and those of the Spaniards had been absent. Now, however, as Alcatraz began to slow down and the military population began to shrink and with the relative quiet of the island returning, those tales of strange sounds and unusual creatures were again coming to the fore.

A permanent prison was still a few years away from construction, and with all of the guns being removed from Alcatraz, the military personnel stationed on the island had very little to do. There were still military prisoners, but their number was not extensive and they were relatively easy to control. This allowed the soldiers plenty of time to wander about the island when not on duty and even more time for their minds to wander. One of the first accounts came in 1902 when a trooper reported hearing drums while on watch. The trooper said he investigated the sound and followed it down to the parade grounds. He said that the sound was loud and steady, and he was wondering why no one else had come to investigate it themselves. The trooper stated that as he approached the parade grounds, the drums got louder and louder until he reached the area where he thought the drums were coming from. He said that he cautiously walked onto the parade grounds, and the second his foot hit the dirt, the drums suddenly stopped. The man looked around the grounds but found no one and never heard the drums beating again.

Another story was told by a captain who was making his rounds of the island late at night. He was checking on his sentries and was approaching the docks when he heard the sound of drums coming from the area of the docks. The captain knew that his men were sometimes bored while on night sentry duty and might have been playing a prank on him. He knew his men respected him and his rank, but this would not be the first time they had played a joke on him. The captain strode down to the dock, certain he would find his sentries laughing, but instead, as soon as he approached the wharf, the drumming ceased. The trooper on sentry duty turned as the captain approached, gave the man a salute and then turned back toward the ocean and resumed his duty. When the captain asked the trooper about the drumming, the man gave his superior a quizzical look and told him he hadn't heard a thing other than the waves lapping the shore all night.

Perhaps the strangest tale told about the phantom drummers comes from the time when Alcatraz was a federal prison. During World War II, Alcatraz was being used as a torpedo and mine storage location. After a late-night restocking ship had dropped off a new supply of ordnance, five men were

Part of the Citadel basement now called the Dungeon.

stacking and storing the new torpedoes when they all began to hear the sound of drums. The men thought this unusual and took a break from their task to go see what was going on. The sound was coming from nearby at the docks, and they wondered if the scow that had made the delivery had turned back to the wharf and was playing some odd drum music over the radio. As they approached the docks, they began to hear the sound of chanting that was in unison with the drumming. When they rounded a corner, what they saw made them stop dead in their tracks. There in front of them was a campfire. The drumming was coming from a group of Indians sitting around the fire, while others danced around the fire pit in time to the beat. The men looked at one another in bewilderment but knew that no one was supposed to be down here, and most assuredly they were not allowed to have a fire this close to a wooden dock. The soldiers started to move forward to tell the Native Americans that they were violating federal law by being on Alcatraz, but before they took three steps, the entire scene vanished before their eyes. According to one trooper, the only reason they reported the incident was to make sure they didn't get in trouble for leaving their assigned task.

The legends of the phantom drums and drummers would start to come in more frequently as the war ended and the military ended all use of the island. Over the years, guards and prisoners alike have reported hearing the drums playing, and the dancers have been seen by both prison guards and park rangers after the prison was closed down. Prisoners have even seen Native Americans walking in the halls and corridors of the prison itself. It is thought that these apparitions are the residuals left by the Native Americans who used the island as a place of exile and ceremony to the evil spirits.

Another legend told about Alcatraz is that of hearing the sounds of gunfire and cannon shot. Over the years following the Civil War, soldiers stationed on the island have reported that while on sentry duty late at night, they thought that Alcatraz was under attack. They would suddenly hear the sound of intense gunfire coming from the island, as if the gunners were shooting at a passing ship or invasion fleet. The alarmed guards would hear not only the cannons but the sound of battle as well: men screaming and running to their posts and ammunition carts being moved into position. The startled guards would hurry from their assigned posts to man their battle positions only to find the island peaceful and the sounds vanished.

This legend has persisted to this day. Park rangers, docents and visitors alike have commented on hearing the same sounds every time it is reported—sounds of men running and screaming, cannons firing and battle commencing and then followed by silence. It ends as abruptly as it begins.

We are a bit confused by this legend because Alcatraz never actually saw battle since its time as a fort from the Spanish occupation through today. Why there would be phantom battle sounds is a complete mystery. The only theory we could come up with has to do with the centennial event of July 4, 1876. All of San Francisco and the surrounding cities were celebrating. The military had planned a "battle" at the Presidio, a naval bombardment of a target floating in the bay, and Alcatraz was to fire four of its guns at the cliffs at Lime Point. When the guns from Alcatraz fired, fragments of the wooden sabot, which was tied around the shells, along with unburned powder from the charges rained down on the men of the lower guns. A piece of burning wood brushed past the shirt of one crewman, setting it on fire, while another came very close to hitting the head of a noncommissioned officer. Neither of the men was seriously hurt, but the frightening effect must have caused the crew great distress.

While the burning embers were falling on the gun crews, a group of military prisoners broke out of their cells and made their way to the commanding officers' reception room. There they stole a quantity of liquor. The men proceeded to get drunk before being apprehended, but the breakout did scare many of the gathered guests who were watching the events from the roof of the Citadel.

This, of course, is just a theory and in no way is to take away from the legend that has grown over the years about this spectral battle. It is simply put here for one's edification.

Another legend that has been furthered once the United States took over stewardship of Alcatraz is that of the red-eyed monster, or what has come to be known as "the Thing." The tales that have come from many of the soldiers, prisoners, guards and rangers over the years are the same as those told when the Spaniards were doing the telling. Even today, reports of a red-eyed animal come in on a semiregular basis. Whether it is Bigfoot, the Bukwus or some other animal that inhabits the island, this seems to be Alcatraz's most enduring legend.

Between 1899 and 1900, the prison population grew from 25 to 441 convicts. To help house these new arrivals, a new prison was quickly built on the parade grounds in early 1900. These wooden cell houses were firetraps, and in 1902, an oil lantern set the lower prison on fire. When the 1906 earthquake struck San Francisco, 175 prisoners from the city jail were transferred to Alcatraz due to the firestorms, and it became clear that the island needed new, fire-resistant buildings to house the growing prison population.

A photograph of Alcatraz pre-1900. *Courtesy of the National Park Service.*

The army began construction on a new concrete barracks that would be built above the casements of the old bombproof barracks. This new building structure would be built by the prisoners, and the infantry soldiers would be replaced by military prison guards. Alcatraz would also be re-designated the "Pacific Branch, U.S. Military Prison, Alcatraz Island." Along with the new barracks, the Citadel was torn down and a huge cell house was built over the basement and moat. This cell house complex would feature a dining hall, hospital, kitchen, recreation yard and four cellblocks that would accommodate six hundred cells. When this was completed in 1912, it was the largest reinforced concrete building in the world.

In 1915, as a way of softening the image of the military prison, Alcatraz underwent another name change. This new designation was subtle: "Pacific Branch, U.S. Disciplinary Barracks." Officials hoped it would better portray the image of military obedience and loyalty that the prison strove to achieve.

Even though the prisoners did the bulk of the labor required on the island, the army soon realized that logistically, Alcatraz was a problem to keep supplied. Food, water and all other supplies had to be imported onto the island by boat, and as such, it became very costly. When the Great Depression struck, things got even worse financially for the Defense Department. That, coupled with the ongoing negative publicity that the island was receiving, convinced the army to close down Alcatraz.

Once it had been decided to close the disciplinary barracks, most of the prisoners were sent to Fort Leavenworth. However, thirty-two of the worst were kept at Alcatraz, and when the army left, the island turned these over

One of the many passageways and storage areas that crisscross the old fortress.

Alcatraz at the turn of the century. *Courtesy of the National Park Service.*

to the Bureau of Prisons. The once mighty fortress of Alcatraz was now part of the federal prison system. The Citadel was covered over by the cell house but would be used as a place of punishment. For all the sordid history of the island up to this point, Alcatraz would know its greatest fame—or infamy—from this point until its transformation into a tourist attraction. For here is where the tales of desperate men and legendary killers would forever set Alcatraz as America's Devil's Island and the infamous inescapable Rock.

CHAPTER 4
ESCAPE FROM ALCATRAZ

Alcatraz claims that no one has ever escaped from the prison—at least, escaped alive. This might not actually be the case, but many inmates have indeed tried to get away from what some have called "America's Devil's Island." Could anyone really blame them? Alcatraz was the place America sent the worst of the worst of its criminals. It might have had the best food in the prison system, but that couldn't make up for the rules of silence, forced labor in the prison workshops or the violence of the inmates toward one another. Add the fact that the prisoners could see the beautiful San Francisco skyline gleaming across the water, and you had the perfect recipe for the need to escape.

Over the twenty-nine years that the Rock was in operation, there were fourteen escape attempts. Twenty-three inmates were caught, two drowned in the rugged tide waters of the San Francisco Bay and six others were shot and killed. There are also five prisoners whose fate is still unclear, but prison records list them as "missing and presumed dead."

JOSEPH "DUTCH" BOWERS (AZ210)

April 26, 1936: Serving twenty-five years for postal mail robbery that netted him $16.38, Joe Bowers found doing time in Alcatraz unbearable. His entire defense during trial was that of need. He told the jury, "I was completely desperate, out of funds, hungry and unable to afford food or lodging." The jury didn't care and found him guilty of all charges.

Being one of the first group of prisoners after Alcatraz opened as a federal prison, Bowers found the strict rules and hardened criminals he was locked up with unacceptable. Warden Johnston said of Bowers, "I did not class him with the shrewd gangsters with whom he associated in prison. He was a weak-minded man with a strong back."

Many believed Bowers to be criminally insane, and his attempted suicide—if it was indeed a legitimate attempt—may be proof of his insanity. The prison psychiatrist, Edward Twitchell, said of Bowers trying to cut his own throat, "The attempts at suicide have been theatrically planned and have resulted in very little damage to him....I believe the unsuccessful attempts were for the purpose of gaining opinion favorable to him."

Whether or not Bowers was sincere in his suicide tries, he had finally had enough of Alcatraz and decided that, one way or another, it was time for him to leave the island. At 11:20 a.m., as the bell sounded for the inmates to return to the cellblock and prepare for lunch, Bowers started walking toward the Model Industries Building and then suddenly ran for the fence. As he climbed the chain link, the road tower guard yelled for him to stop and get down from the fence, but Bowers ignored all of his warnings. Seeing that Bowers was about to go over the fence, the officer took aim and fired two shots from his service rifle, striking Bowers and causing him to lurch over the chain link and fall to the shoreline below. Bowers was only forty years old when he died violently, as criminals often do.

There have been reports over the years by both guards and passing boaters of a spectral figure who wanders the rugged shoreline where Bowers met his end. Could this wandering spirit be the inmate still reveling in his freedom? If one can call it that.

THEODORE COLE (AZ258) AND RALPH ROE (AZ260)

December 16, 1937: Theodore Cole was as bad as one could be. He started his life of crime at the tender age of eleven and killed his first victim, an Arkansas police officer, at age fourteen. By the age of twenty, he had been sentenced to die in the electric chair and subsequently had his conviction dropped to fifteen years. While in prison, Cole admitted to stabbing his cellmate twenty-seven times, resulting in his death, but called it self-defense. While awaiting trial on those charges, Cole managed to escape and was off and running on his newest crime spree.

A few weeks after Cole escaped from prison, he kidnapped a merchant, hoping to score a big ransom, but instead was arrested in Dallas, Texas, and sent back to Oklahoma to face federal kidnapping charges. The entire time he was in custody awaiting trial, he tried escaping several times, once by cutting through the bars and hiding in a trash can. He even managed to slip out of his manacles. One reporter described Cole as "an eel-like little man." Cole was sentenced to fifty years and sent to Alcatraz as a way of preventing him from ever escaping custody again.

Ralph Roe, although not quite as vicious or deliberate as Cole, was a convicted bank robber and murderer with a couple of escape attempts under his belt as well, prompting a federal judge to label him an escape risk and thereby relegating him to the Rock to prevent him from fleeing custody. The two escape artists met on Alcatraz, and the planning commenced.

While working in the Model Industries Building, Roe and Cole discovered that the flat iron bars installed in the window could be filed enough to allow them to be removed. Over time, the two men slowly made headway, disguising their work by using shoe polish mixed with the grease they used working in the tire repair shop. Once they had loosened enough of the bars to fit their bodies through, they waited until the right conditions arose before making their move to leave the island.

On December 16, as a severe storm arose over San Francisco Bay and a thick fog rolled in behind it, the men made their way out of the barred window. Obscured by the storm, the two men ran toward a fence, made their way past this obstacle, jumped the twenty or so feet to the churning maelstrom of the sea below—and vanished into obscurity.

Once it had been discovered that the prisoners were missing, the manhunt began. When no trace of the two were found on the island, boats were dispatched to search the surrounding waters, but with the seas as rough as they were, it was pretty clear that any attempt to swim to shore was all but futile. Theodore Cole and Ralph Roe were officially listed as "missing and presumed dead," and the manhunt was called off.

There is some speculation, as there always is, that the men survived their flight. It is believed that the inmates had secreted tires they had somehow managed to slip out of the Industries Building and had used those as floatation devices to help them escape. Using these "rafts," Cole and Roe survived the waters and resumed their lives of crime. One can see how this might be a product of urban legend, but the logistics of the men getting tires past the guards, down a twenty-foot drop and safe from the tides while waiting for the right conditions make this theory a bit wet.

JOE CRETZER (AZ548), LLOYD BARKDOLL (AZ423), ARNOLD KYLE (AZ547) AND SAM SHOCKLEY (AZ462)

May 21, 1941: While working in the Model Industries Building, these four inmates hatched a plan to pry open a window and escape while prisoners and guards were returning from lunch. They thought that the mild confusion of the crowd would help mask their escape.

The convicts hurried back to their assigned area, the mat shop, and shortly after they arrived, they lured guard Clyne Stoops to the work area by telling him that a machine had broken down. They overpowered Stoops and yard officer Lionel Johnston, tied their hands and legs with twine, gagged them and then began prying the window open with a piece of pipe. While they were working on the window, Superintendent of Industries C.J. Manning walked in for a routine inspection and caught the inmates in their attempt. Before he could flee and raise the alarm, he was also overpowered and bound hand and foot like the other guards. Manning, however, wasn't gagged.

Still struggling with the window, the four escapees dragged over a motorized grinding stone in the hopes it could cut through the bars. While their attention was turned toward their task, Guard Captain Madigan

The Model Industries Building as it sits today.

walked into the shop and surprised the inmates, and a brief struggle ensued before the four escapees managed to subdue Madigan.

After tying up the captain, the convicts went back to work but were still having trouble getting the window open. As they were working on opening their escape route, Madigan and Manning were telling the inmates that it wouldn't be long before the guards were found missing and the captain was due to call in after his inspection. Once Madigan was found to be late, the alarm would sound, and the guards would then arm themselves in the search for the missing captain and guards. They told the convicts that their only hope of getting out of this alive or, at the very least, without a massive amount of time added to their sentence on Alcatraz was to give themselves up. After the four inmates huddled together to talk, they came to the realization that they weren't going to be able to escape. They freed their captives and surrendered without further incident. The entire attempt lasted two hours.

This would not be the last time these inmates tried to escape. Their next attempt would become the bloodiest chapter in Alcatraz history and a legend of infamy.

JOHN BAYLESS (AZ466)

September 15, 1941: John Bayless liked to keep to himself. He didn't want to draw attention and certainly didn't want to get on the bad side of any of the other prisoners. He wasn't what one would call an ideal inmate; but he also wasn't one to get into too much trouble either. As such, Bayless pretty much flew under everyone's radar. This may be why his actions in September 1941 came as a surprise.

While on garbage duty, Bayless gazed over at the San Francisco skyline and thought about freedom. As he looked, an unexpected thick fog drifted over the island, and Bayless, seeing a chance to attain that freedom, used the heavy mist to sneak down to the waterline and begin swimming for the mainland. Bayless never thought about the water temperature, and as he swam farther out, the extreme cold began affecting his ability to move. John Bayless began to flounder, and as he attempted to swim back to Alcatraz, he knew he was going to drown in the frigid waters of the bay. He was pulled to safety by the guards just as hypothermia set in. The guards had heard him calling for help. A few months later, after he had recovered from his impromptu swim, Bayless was sent to the city to stand trial for his escape attempt. While awaiting the judge's return to the courtroom, Bayless bolted for the door, again trying for freedom. He didn't even make it to the doors before the bailiff and another court officer apprehended him. For his two escape attempts, the judge added five years to his sentence on the Rock.

JAMES BOARMAN (AZ571), HAROLD BREST (AZ380 & AZ487), FLOYD HAMILTON (AZ523) AND FRED HUNTER (AZ402)

April 14, 1943: These four inmates had a similar idea to that of Cretzer, Barkdoll, Kyle and Shockley. The difference here was that they already knew they could get out of the window in the Model Industries Building. So the convicts made homemade knives, or "shivs," and using these, they took Officer Smith, bound and gagged him and headed for the window that would lead them to freedom. Unfortunately, Captain Weinhold was making his rounds and noticed Smith wasn't where he was supposed to be. He went into the room and was captured too. While the captain was being tied up and gagged, the other inmates managed to get the window open, and the four men stripped down to their underwear, covered themselves in thick grease, ran to the nearby cliff and leapt thirty feet down into the frigid water. The inmates had previously filled four cans with army uniforms, sealed the cans and had planned on using them as floatation aids; unfortunately, two of the cans had been left behind, and none of them knew whose uniforms were missing.

While the convicts made their way to the cliff face, Officer Smith somehow managed to free his whistle and get it into Captain Weinhold's mouth. At the same time the whistle sounded, Officer Frank Johnson, who was stationed outside, spotted the near-naked inmates and sounded the alarm. The tower guards, seeing the convicts jump into the bay, waited until they cleared the cliff, and once they were in view, they opened fire on the four men. Boarman had been knocked unconscious in the jump, and Brest had been holding on to him. As a prison launch pulled up next to the two men, Brest let go of Boarman. The guards on the small boat assumed that Boarman had been killed and let him slip under water; his body was never recovered.

Hunter had injured his back when he hit the water and cut his hands on the rocks nearby. These injuries made it extremely hard for him to swim, and he finally gave up and tried to hide in a nearby cave. The guards in a second launch had seen him enter the cave and positioned their boat at the entrance. After repeated calls for Hunter to come out were ignored, the guards fired a pistol round into the cave opening, prompting Hunter to surrender.

No sign could be found of Floyd Hamilton, and he was assumed dead by the prison. Warden James Johnston went so far as to put out a statement saying, "We're positive that Hamilton is dead. He was shot and we saw him go under."

Hamilton was far from dead. As Hunter had entered the cave, he found that Hamilton was already hiding there and, being first, had taken the only spot safe from randomly fired bullets. When Hunter left the cave, Hamilton stayed behind and waited for three days before leaving the relative safety. On Friday night, Hamilton climbed back up the cliff and went through the same window that he had escaped from. Once back inside the Model Industries Building, he hid under a pile of materials in a storeroom until he was discovered there the following morning. Hamilton was completely unharmed by the entire escapade.

HURON WALTERS (AZ536)

August 7, 1943: Huron Walters was an Arkansas bank robber, car thief and assaulter who was doing thirty years on Alcatraz rather than Leavenworth because he had already tried once to escape from prison. He also decided to try his luck at getting off the Rock—not always a smart or easy task.

Walters was assigned to work in the prison laundry, a job he couldn't stand. He had complained to other inmates that he wanted to get out of that job, but so far, he hadn't been successful at convincing the guards or warden to switch his assignment. It might have been his hatred of the laundry room, or just his desire to be free, that prompted Walters to sneak out through a laundry room door and make a play for freedom. Whatever the reason, once outside, Walters headed for the beach on the Golden Gate side of the island and attempted to get in the water and swim for the mainland. We say attempted because once Walters realized just how cold the San Francisco Bay was, he had second thoughts.

Once Walters turned up missing, the alarm was sounded, and an all-out manhunt ensued. Five Coast Guard vessels joined the prison boats searching the waters for Walters, but no sign of him was found. While the boats powered around the island, prison guards scoured the shoreline and finally found Walters hiding among some rocks on the beach opposite the laundry room door he had snuck through. He was returned to his cell and his laundry job, but with a few more years of time added on to his sentence.

JOHN GILES (AZ250)

July 31, 1945: Patience is a virtue and one that can help when planning an escape from an inescapable island prison. Virtue is not something generally associated with criminals, but John Giles had patience in droves.

Giles was serving a life sentence for murder at an Oregon prison before he escaped. On May 11, 1935, he was convicted of the attempted robbery of the Denver and Rio Grande Western mail train. He spent a brief time at McNeil Island prison before being sent to Alcatraz due to his escape record. Once on the Rock, he was assigned to the work detail on the dock, where he helped load and unload the army laundry sent to Alcatraz. At this time, Alcatraz had been commissioned to wash all of the local army base's laundry. Giles, seeing the uniforms, hatched an idea for escape but knew that it would take time to implement.

Over the next few years, Giles would find bits and pieces of the uniforms that were his size and steal them and hide them, knowing that no one would notice a shirt here, a pair of pants there going missing. The trick was to only steal a piece infrequently. Giles was correct, and he managed to obtain a complete uniform over time. Then, it was only a matter of waiting for his opportunity to make his move.

Giles always kept his purloined uniform close at hand while at work on the docks, and when the army ferry *USAT General Frank M. Coxe* tied up at

John Giles snuck aboard a transport from these docks thinking he was heading for freedom. He was actually heading for a longer prison term.

the Alcatraz dock, he knew it was time to leave the island. Donning the army uniform, Giles snuck aboard the ferry and down through a freight hatchway. Giles found a group of men mingling about and joined them as if he belonged on the boat. As the boat pulled away from the dock, a sergeant did a head count and was confused to find that he had one extra soldier aboard. Back on Alcatraz, a routine head count of the prisoners was made to prevent exactly the type of escape attempt that was occurring. It showed that they were down one inmate. Assistant Warden E.J. Miller immediately hopped on a speedboat and began following the army ferry while prison officials radioed ahead to let Fort McDowell know that an escape was in progress.

John Giles had assumed that the boat he had hitched a ride on was headed to San Francisco. Unfortunately for him, the boat was actually headed for the army base on Angel Island. Giles, thinking he had been successful in his attempt, chatted it up with the other passengers, who thought he was a lineman working on the cable. Giles had come up with this story on the fly, but everyone bought it. Once the ferry tied up at the dock on Angel Island, Giles just blended into the crowd of soldiers but was detained by a lieutenant for a disorderly uniform and was still trying to talk his way past the eagle-eyed officer when Miller, accompanied by several prison guards, appeared and took Giles into custody. Giles arrived back on Alcatraz by 11:00 a.m.

FLOYD WILSON (AZ956)

July 26, 1956: Floyd Wilson was a small-time crook who murdered a Washington, D.C. store clerk and was serving a life sentence on Alcatraz when he decided one day to just walk away from his job on the island's dock.

Since Alcatraz was an island with no natural resources, not even water, everything that the prison needed had to be brought in by boat or barge. As such, manual labor was required to offload everything. Since the island was full of prisoners, they were used as this manual labor force. Floyd Wilson was one of the prisoners who loaded and offloaded the supplies at the docks.

Wilson was helping pump the 250,000 gallons of water onto the island from the barge assigned that day, and when finished, army Tug3 *T-893* departed the island pushing the now empty water barge. As the tug pulled away from the dock, the prisoners, as they always did, stood on a painted line for a head count. It was quickly discovered that Wilson was missing. Prison officials immediately called ahead to Fort Mason's Pier 3, where the tug was searched thoroughly, but Wilson was not found to be aboard.

Once it was clear that Wilson hadn't caught a ride with the tug, a foot by foot search was launched on the island itself, but there was still no sign of the missing prisoner. The search continued for twelve hours until low tide revealed Wilson hiding among some rocks near the island seawall. Once prison guards approached, the shivering Wilson gave up without a struggle.

AARON BURGETT (AZ991) AND CLYDE JOHNSON (AZ864)

September 29, 1958: Aaron Burgett was a young, small-time crook doing twenty-five years on Alcatraz for a post office robbery and other violent armed robberies in Missouri. Clyde Johnson, on the other hand, was a forty-year-old career criminal who had once escaped from the twenty-one-story Dade County jail in Miami, Florida, which gave him his ticket to the Rock for the next forty years.

Assigned to the clean-up and garbage detail, the two convicts were escorted out beyond the fence line on occasion to do work. This gave the two men an idea for escape, especially while staring at the tempting view of the San Francisco skyline so deceptively close by. Once the idea struck, the planning began.

On a bright, sunny September day, while working along the Alcatraz shoreline picking up trash, Johnson pulled out a hidden knife and threatened their lone, unarmed guard with death if he didn't surrender to them. The guard, Harold Miller, was a six-foot, two-inch-tall young man who had been working at the prison for less than a year. The inmates restrained Miller, bound and gagged him with electrical tape and then blindfolded him before tying him to a tree with rope they had hidden from view.

The two convicts had made crude wooden "swim fins" to attach to their shoes and had hidden small plastic bags under their clothes that they inflated to use as flotation aids for their swim to the mainland. The two inmates made their way down to the rocky shore and tried to enter into the roiling waters but found it almost impossible. Johnson realized that the danger was too great and gave up. Burgett, knowing that their attack on Miller along with the escape attempt meant many more years added to his already long sentence, made the drastic decision to jump. Once in the rough waters, he began thrashing around but managed to make slow progress toward the waiting San Francisco shoreline.

When Officer Miller failed to report in on schedule, other guards went looking for him and his two charges. They found Miller where Johnson and Burgett had left him, and once Miller told them what had happened, they raised the alarm. Johnson was found almost at once hiding behind some bushes near the tree where they had tied their hapless guard and surrendered without incident. Once the other prisoners were secured in their cells, the rest of the Alcatraz guards scoured the island, and the Coast Guard, along with the prison launches, began searching the waters of the bay. No sign of Aaron Burgett was found in the days that the search went on.

As the week stretched into two, the fate of Burgett became the topic of not only those on Alcatraz but in the mainland population as well. The escape-proof maximum-security prison wasn't as secure as everyone thought. Burgett had managed to escape the Rock. The inmates knew that no one had ever come close but figured if anyone was to be the first, it would be the young man from Nebraska. The mood in the cellblock was almost festive at the thought—that is, until something was spotted floating near the shore in the area where Burgett had taken his plunge for freedom.

After fourteen days missing, Aaron Burgett's body was spotted bumping up against the rocks of the island, moving with the tide. Once his corpse was hauled onto land, the prison doctors knew what had happened. Burgett had apparently been dragged under the waves as he had tried to swim the rough waters, with the strong tides keeping his body on the bottom of the bay. His corpse was "eaten full of holes," as one guard said, most likely from the crabs that inhabit the sea floor. Part of the homemade wooden fins was still attached to his shoes, and his inmate number, 991, was still visible on his shirt. Aaron Burgett had not been the first to escape America's Devil's Island.

JOHN PAUL SCOTT (AZ1403) AND DARL PARKER (AZ1413)

December 16, 1962: John Scott was serving thirty years for bank robbery and firearms charges. Darl Parker was serving fifty years for bank robbery and kidnapping. Both men had a history of escape attempts, and both men had said that given the chance, they would try again—even if it meant swimming

This guard tower commanded a superb view if a prisoner tried to enter the water as a means of escape.

the treacherous waters of San Francisco Bay. When the two were assigned together on culinary duty, they hatched a plan to do just that.

Over a few weeks' time, Scott and Parker had been working on cutting through the bars on the window in the cell house kitchen basement. Once they had cut enough to bend the bars the rest of the way by hand, they figured it was time to make a break for freedom. At 5:30 p.m. on that cold December night, the two men climbed out through the window and made their way down to the water's edge. Before entering the water, Parker and Scott put on "water-wings" they had made using surgical gloves and prison shirts. Almost immediately upon entering the bay, both men began struggling in the frigid waters.

Both convicts realized that they could never make it to San Francisco and tried to swim back to the prison. Parker managed to get back to a small rock outcropping known as "Little Alcatraz," and that is where authorities would later find him. Scott, however, was caught in the strong current and was being pulled out to sea. Parker watched as he disappeared from view, knowing he had seen the last of his friend.

Once the alarm was sounded and a search begun, it didn't take long for Parker to be picked up by the prison launch. Darl Parker told the guards what had happened to Scott, and the Coast Guard was notified to begin searching for his body. A few hours after the search began, a call came in that a body had been found by teenagers on the rocks near Fort Point under the Golden Gate Bridge. The Coast Guard arrived to recover the body but found that Scott was still alive, albeit barely. Scott was taken to the Presidio army base hospital and treated for shock and hypothermia. By 11:00 p.m., Scott was on his way back to his prison cell.

This was the last escape attempt to take place at the prison. Just three months after this escape, Alcatraz closed. In the twenty-nine years that Alcatraz was a federal prison, fourteen escape attempts occurred. It was always said that the island was escape proof because of the strong currents, cold water and man-eating sharks (in actuality, there are only bottom-dwelling sharks) that inhabit the bay. On the last desperate try for freedom from the Rock, John Paul Scott proved it could be done. If Scott could make it alive, one must wonder if any of the other "missing and presumed dead" inmates might have made it as well.

CHAPTER 5

THE GREAT ESCAPES

M uch has been said about the escape attempts at Alcatraz Prison. Most of the time the attempts, while not peaceful, at the very least were mild compared to some of the more spectacular tries. Yes, some of the other escapes resulted in the deaths of inmates, but the tales within this chapter show just how cold, calculating and vicious another human being can be when faced with captivity at the hands of another—even when that captivity is fully warranted.

THOMAS LIMERICK (AZ263), JIMMY LUCAS (AZ224) AND RUFUS FRANKLIN (AZ335)

May 23, 1938: Thomas Limerick may have never turned to crime if his father hadn't died, leaving his family in severe poverty when he was just fifteen years old. Unfortunately, his father did die, and Tom turned to robbing boxcars, which turned into bank robbery and finally a National Guard armory. Limerick was arrested in May 1935 and sentenced to life in prison.

Serving thirty years in federal prison for bank robbery and auto theft, James "Tex" Lucas also had detainers in his home state of Texas that totaled 128 years. These charges included robbery, murder and escape. He was only 22 years old when he was sent to Alcatraz.

Being a prisoner was hard. But working in the Model Industries Building could be even worse.

Lucas was a troublemaker once he arrived on the island. He helped instigate a work strike in 1936, was known to participate in all sorts of off-limits activities and even attempted to kill Al Capone in the showers with half a pair of scissors. When asked why he tried to kill Capone, all Lucas would say was, "Well, he threatened to kill me." This act raised respect for him from the other prisoners but also put him squarely in the sights of the warden and guards for close scrutiny from that moment on.

Alabama-born Rufus "Whitey" Franklin was a convicted bank robber, car thief and violent man who was repeatedly jailed for assault. Franklin spent almost his entire life behind bars, and when he was finally paroled from an Atlanta prison in 1974, he died from lung cancer shortly thereafter. He almost seemed as if he was a reformed man. Even his warden believed that Rufus had changed his ways. Besides his violent and deadly escape attempt, Franklin has the dubious distinction of spending the longest term in a closed solitary cell of any inmate at Alcatraz.

The escape was planned by Limerick and Lucas while working in the Model Industries Building. The two realized that they could gain access to the roof from the woodworking shop and decided that May 23 was the day for the attempt. One of the inmates grabbed a hammer from the shop and struck unarmed officer Royal Cline repeatedly, beating the man to death. The three then made their way to the roof and tried to assault the guard tower in an attempt to get Officer Harold Stites's rifle. Before the convicts could close the distance, however, Stites took aim and fired, killing Limerick and wounding Franklin. Lucas then surrendered and was taken into custody.

Lucas and Franklin were charged with murder and sentenced to life in prison. Both were placed in solitary confinement in D block, most likely as revenge for killing one of the officers' own. Lucas received a presidential commutation and was released from prison. Stites received praise for his quick action in apprehending the three inmates and returned to duty unharmed. He was later killed in a prison riot in 1946.

Over the years after this escape attempt, many of the guards manning the tower on the roof have reported seeing what looks like a prisoner trying to cross the roof toward them. They say that as the inmate nears the tower, he simply disappears. Even to this day, boaters, tourists and rangers report seeing this prisoner crossing Alcatraz's roof before fading from view. Could this specter be Thomas Limerick reliving his moment of death over and over?

ARTHUR "DOC" BARKER (AZ268), DALE STAMPHILL (AZ435), WILLIAM MARTIN (AZ370), RUFUS MCCAIN (AZ267) AND HENRI YOUNG (AZ244)

January 13, 1939: Arthur "Doc" Barker was a member of the Bloody Barker Gang and the son of the now infamous Ma Barker. Barker was a ruthless man and had no use for the law. He and his three brothers committed numerous crimes throughout the early 1900s, including car theft, robbery and murder. Arrested in 1918, Barker escaped and went right back to his criminal ways. Then, in 1921, Barker and three other men robbed a woman at a hospital construction site but were surprised by the night watchman, who opened fire on the four criminals but was killed himself when they fired back. Barker was convicted of the watchman's murder and sentenced to life in prison. Barker appealed his conviction and was paroled in September 1932.

It didn't take Doc long to team up with his brothers again and, along with friend Alvin Karpis, form the Barker-Karpis gang. After a string of deadly robberies and bank heists, Barker was again arrested, convicted on kidnapping charges and sentenced to life in prison. This time, however, Barker and his friend Karpis were sent to Alcatraz. It would be his last stop.

Dale Stamphill was said to be the mastermind of this escape attempt and is the one who acquired the saws that the inmates used to cut through the flat iron bars of their cells in D block. Stamphill also concocted the wax mixture used to hide the cut marks from the guards to keep the attempt a secret from those in charge on Alcatraz.

William "Ty" Martin was a post office robber sentenced to Alcatraz at a time when black criminals were treated quite differently than their white counterparts. Racism was running wild in America, and it was no different in the prison system. Doc Barker, though, saw something in Martin that he liked, and Ty became Doc's enforcer while on Alcatraz; therefore, he was automatically included in the escape attempt.

Rufus McCain was a bank robber sentenced to ninety-nine years in prison. McCain and another man had robbed a bank in Idabel, Oklahoma, when a bank clerk recognized McCain. McCain and his accomplice kidnapped two of the bank clerks as hostages in case they needed them, but as the robbery was in progress, armed citizens had gathered outside the bank and fired on the group coming out of the door. In the gun battle that ensued, McCain's accomplice, Sam Day, was pelted with buckshot in the right shoulder, prompting the two robbers to surrender. Day would later die from his injuries. When McCain was sentenced by the jury, the judge in the case was outraged that he was not sentenced to death and rebuked the jury for its decision yet didn't overturn the sentence. Rufus McCain would never leave Alcatraz alive.

Henri Young was another one of those criminals who should never have been allowed in civilized society. Born in 1911 to a poor family, Young decided that bank robbing was preferable to hard work and went about the business of theft with relish. Young was well known for taking hostages during his robberies and didn't care if they got hurt or killed as long as they served their purpose. Young was finally caught and convicted of murder and sent to prison in Washington State and Montana before being sent to Alcatraz.

Doc Barker had enough of Alcatraz and wanted out, at any cost. He had been talking to Dale Stamphill about a possible escape plan and told Stamphill to start preparing. With the word given, Stamphill began forming copper into saw blades they would use to cut through the flat metal bars on the D block doors. Stamphill also managed to jerry-rig a makeshift bar spreader they would need for the cellblock window leading to the outside world. Over a period of time, the five men were able to cut through the bars, hiding the cuts using a concoction of wax and black paint. After all of the bars were ready, all that was left was to wait for the right weather to roll into San Francisco Bay and it would be time to escape.

On the night of January 12, the fog rolled thickly into the bay and surrounded Alcatraz in a blanket of white. Just after the 3:00 a.m. watch passed by their cells, the five convicts pried loose their precut bars and slipped through the narrow openings and into the main cellblock corridor. They then carefully and as silently as possible used the homemade bar spreader and dropped down eight feet to the dirt below. Once outside, the inmates separated, with Barker and Stamphill making their way down to an alcove where they began collecting driftwood for their flotation device. Martin, McCain and Young headed to the docks to find lumber to tie together for their raft.

While spreading the bars on the outside window, the convicts had caused a popping noise, but most of the guards ignored it, thinking it was an inmate trying to stop a neighbor from snoring. This noise caught the attention of Junior Officer Hurst. Hurst didn't think the noise was anything to worry about at first and so didn't immediately investigate. It took him almost half an hour before he decided to walk D block just in case there was something amiss. While passing Dale Stamphill's cell, the guard noticed the bars missing from the lower section of the door and promptly raised the alarm.

While Junior Officer Hurst was looking at the missing bars of the cell door, McCain, Young and Martin were launching their haphazardly put together raft and paddling out into the fog-shrouded waters of the bay. As they got farther from the island, McCain began to get more agitated. The other two convicts noticed but didn't say anything. As the water got deeper and deeper, McCain started to panic and informed Young and Martin that he couldn't swim. McCain was so twitchy that he threatened to overturn the tiny, rickety raft, and this forced the three to turn back to Alcatraz. When the escapees reached the docks that they had just left, the prison guards were waiting for them, and they surrendered without a fight.

Doc Barker and Dale Stamphill had made their way down to a small cove where they were fashioning a crude raft to act as an aid while they tried to swim to freedom. They had not finished by the time a launch boat passed by and illuminated the two with a searchlight. The inmates were ordered to raise their hands, but neither of them did so in a timely manner, and the guards on the launch opened fire on them. Both Stamphill and Barker were hit in the legs by multiple rifle rounds and went down in the rocks that were strewn over the beach. Again, they were told to raise their hands. Stamphill immediately surrendered, but Barker was in so much pain from the leg wounds that he tried to stand up to relieve the pain and was shot just below the right eye. Barker lived a few hours more before dying from his head wound.

Stamphill and Martin were sent to the hospital for injuries they received during the escape. All four of the prisoners had their prison time extended and were sent into solitary confinement in the "hole." After being released from the isolation cells, Young and McCain both spent a few months in the punishment segregation cells.

In December 1941, while Young and McCain were at work in different areas of the Model Industries Building, Henri Young fashioned a makeshift knife out of a planer blade he used working in the furniture shop. Just after the 10:00 a.m. prisoner count, he ran downstairs to the tailor shop and stabbed McCain in the stomach. Rufus McCain was taken to the hospital ward and, after suffering extreme pain for more than five hours, died of his injuries.

Henri Young was convicted of involuntary manslaughter for the killing. His lawyer used the claim that Young had gone insane due to the torture he received at Alcatraz, along with "cruel and unusual punishment" after the failed escape attempt. These false claims were later used in the movie *Murder in the First*, starring Kevin Bacon. A more plausible explanation

The most notorious cell on Alcatraz, 14D. Rufus McCain not only spent a lot of time here, but he is also said to be the entity who haunts it still.

was that Young, still angry about the failed escape attempt a year earlier, blamed McCain for its failure due to his fear of drowning and had decided to take his revenge.

Rufus McCain's death at the hands of Young was a vicious and painful demise. This type of murder can cause a person's spirit to remain behind in an attempt at retribution or as a way to rectify the pain it felt in passing. McCain, having spent so much time in confinement, especially cell 14D, has been said to be the cause of the extreme haunting of that particular cell.

THE BATTLE OF ALCATRAZ

May 2–4, 1946: This event is known as the bloodiest to happen at Alcatraz prison. So worried were authorities that the situation would get out of hand that they called in the U.S. Marines to quell what they believed was an uprising by the prisoners. In actuality, it was another escape attempt by Sam Shockley, Joe Cretzer and others that was doomed to failure from the very beginning and a bloodbath that could have very easily been avoided.

Joe Cretzer was a bank robber with a mean streak and at one point had reached public enemy no. 4 on the FBI list. Cretzer was serving a twenty-five-year sentence on Alcatraz and had already tried to escape once from the prison in May 1941. Sam Shockley was a convicted kidnapper and bank robber who was serving a life term for his crimes. Shockley had such a low IQ that some people believe he was mentally incompetent and should have been placed in a psychiatric facility rather than the prison system, but his tendency for violent outbursts made the court's decision acceptable. Inmate Jim Quillen (AZ586), in his book *Inside Alcatraz* (Random House, 2016), said of Shockley, "Executing Sam was the equivalent to killing a mentally-ill child.…I believe he was a victim of the break, not a co-conspirator." Shockley had also joined Cretzer in his earlier escape attempt.

The other co-conspirators were Miran Thompson (AZ729), who was serving life plus ninety-nine years for kidnapping and murder; Marvin Hubbard (AZ645); Clarence Carnes (AZ714), who was the youngest inmate to ever be incarcerated at Alcatraz when he entered the prison at the age of eighteen to serve out his life plus ninety-nine years; and Bernard Coy (AZ415), the one believed to have planned the escape attempt. Coy was serving a life sentence for bank robbery when the Battle of Alcatraz began.

Bernard Coy had one of the most sought-after inmate jobs in the prison. He had been assigned to the maintenance department, and this afforded him almost unfettered access to the entire cell house. While working this job, Coy realized that there were certain patterns that he might be able to use to his advantage in escaping the prison. Over a period of several months, Coy noticed that right after lunch, the main cellblock was all but deserted and the guard on duty in the gun gallery never deviated from his normal routine of patrolling the gallery. Coy found five other inmates who were as anxious as he was for freedom, and together they planned exactly how they were going to escape. The fateful day came in the afternoon of a bright May day.

While Coy was sweeping the floor nearby, Marvin Hubbard, who was a kitchen orderly, approached guard William Miller to tell him he was finished with his assignment. While Miller was distracted, Coy crept up behind the guard and attacked him and, with the help of Hubbard, overpowered Miller. Coy then stripped down to his underwear, smeared grease all over his body, climbed up to the west end gun gallery and used a homemade bar spreader to widen the opening. Once Coy had the bars at the proper size, he squeezed his now slippery body through the bars, made his way to the door and waited for the guard's predictable routine. As the guard opened the door, Coy sprang up and slammed the door hard into the guard, throwing

The gun galleries are high above the cellblock floors and not easy to get into from the inmate side of the bars.

the man off balance. Coy then brutally attacked him with a riot club from the gallery and strangled the guard with his own necktie until he passed out.

Coy now had access to a weapons locker and hurriedly lowered riot clubs and a couple of firearms down to Hubbard and Cretzer, who had come over when the escape began. Coy kept the gallery guard's rifle as he made his way back down to the cellblock floor.

Now fully armed, the convicts rounded up the other guards, all of whom were unarmed, and locked them into cells 403 and 404. Knowing that Miller had the keys they needed to get out of the cell house and into the exercise yard and from there to the docks, they demanded that Miller give them up or be killed. Miller did so with no complaint.

After acquiring the keys, the three convicts released Thompson, Shockley and Carnes, and then they threw open all of the other cells in an attempt at getting as many of the inmates as possible to join them. After the other prisoners heard what the escapees had planned, they all returned to their cells. The six convicts now went to work on the exercise yard door. They tried every key on the ring that Miller had given them, but none of them seemed to work. Unbeknownst to the escapees, Officer Miller had managed to remove the outside door key and had hidden it in the toilet of the cell where they had locked him up. By now, however, even if they had the right key, they had tried so many times using the wrong key that the lock was hopelessly jammed.

By this time, prison officials were being told that some of the guards had failed to check in, and other guards were sent to the area. These officers were met at gunpoint by the convicts and were put into the two cells with the other captives. By now the six escapees realized that their original plan was never going to work, and as the wail of sirens sounded moments later, they knew that escape was impossible. Coy went over to the windows facing San Francisco and saw guards gathering at the prison entrance and fired at them with his stolen rifle. While Coy was busy with the gathering guards, Cretzer and the others were worried that the officers they had taken hostage would identify them as the ringleaders, so Cretzer told those convicts with guns to kill the helpless guards. Carnes, wanting no part in the massacre, told the others he wasn't going to do it and went back to his cell. Cretzer, in a fit of rage, opened up with his pistol, blindly firing into the now cringing officers. Neither he nor any of the other convicts took the time to see if the guards were dead but walked away from the locked cell to figure out their next move.

The first assault to take back the prison was led by Lieutenant Phil Bergan. He took his men through the west end gun gallery but found that the inmates had anticipated their move and were waiting for them in ambush. In the hail of gunfire that followed, three guards were hit, and the team was forced to retreat. One of the officers who had been hit was Harold Stites, the officer who had prevented Limerick, Lucas and Franklin from escaping in 1938. Stites would become the first casualty of the Battle of Alcatraz. A second attempt at freeing the hostages and retaking the prison also failed, but this time, the assault team was able to close and secure the D block access door. This meant that the convicts' space to maneuver was greatly restricted. Seeing their chances of coming out of this alive fading, Thompson and Shockley returned to their cells.

When Warden Johnston realized that his men were not going to be able to retake the prison, the Coast Guard and marines were called in to aid the prison guards. As the second assault was taking place, the marines started tossing explosive devices into the cellblock. The prison began to fill with thick smoke, choking the inmates who were not involved and who were hiding under mattresses in an attempt to shield themselves from flying shrapnel and ricocheting bullets.

Inmate Jim Quillian recalled, "It was a savage, all-out attempt to spill convict blood. We lay on the floor behind our mattresses and could hear the bullets thud into them. The bullets started several fires of the mattresses. It was difficult to breathe because of the smoke and tear gas. We lay there for hours, praying we'd not get hit."

The viciousness of the marines' attack even got the attention of Robert Stroud, the infamous "Birdman of Alcatraz," who, at fifty-six years old, allegedly climbed over the railing, lowered himself down to the cellblock floor and began closing the doors of the isolation ward cells to keep the helpless inmates safe from the onslaught. The whole time he was working on the doors, he was calling out to the guards that there were no firearms in D block and to stop firing.

As the battle to retake the prison continued, the marines climbed up to the roof of the main building, drilled holes and began lowering grenades down onto the prison floor in an attempt at getting the inmates to surrender or possibly killing them. In all, approximately five hundred hand grenades were used. The explosions may not have had the desired effect, but they did cause Coy, Cretzer and Hubbard to retreat into one of the utility corridors.

After a few more hours with no return fire coming from the prisoners, a ceasefire was called. Carefully, the marines and prison guards approached the doors and entered the cellblock. What they found was a cell house riddled with bullet holes and pockmarked with shrapnel. The prisoners who

The damage caused by the marines' grenades is still highly visible in this pass-through corridor.

had been caught in the cell house when the battle began were found hiding under mattresses, clothing, blankets or anything else they could find to keep the deadly flying metal from killing them. They were all rounded up and taken to a location to sort out those responsible. Cretzer, Coy and Hubbard were found dead in the utility corridor they had sought refuge in. Coy was found wearing a guard uniform with a rifle nearby. Cretzer was only a few feet away from Coy with a pistol by his side and the cell house keys still in his pocket. Hubbard was found farther down the corridor, away from the other two, and is believed to have been the last to die.

The marines and guards who found the hostages were appalled by the sight that greeted them. They could see the spray of bullet holes dotting both of the cells and hurriedly went to the aid of the injured men. William Miller, the courageous guard who hid the yard key from the escapees, would die from his injuries. Guard Ernest Lageson was shot in the face but managed to write the names of the six escapees and circled the names of the ringleaders: Hubbard, Coy and Cretzer.

Thompson and Shockley would be sent to the gas chamber at San Quentin and sit side by side as the poison took their lives. Carnes was spared the death penalty when guards told how he had refused to take part in the killing of the

The bullet damage from the Battle of Alcatraz can still be seen today on the outside walls of the prison.

hostages but received an additional ninety-nine-year sentence for his part. In all, five people were killed, two guards and three escapees. Eighteen other guards were injured, as well as almost all of the non-participating inmates, to one degree or another. This was indeed the bloodiest and most violent episode in the history of Alcatraz.

Visitors to the prison today can still see the signs of the Battle of Alcatraz. Grenade damage can be seen on the walls and floors of the cellblock, and if one looks closely at the outside walls, some of the bullet marks are still faintly visible. However, the most telltale signs that remain from the battle are the ghosts of Coy, Cretzer and Hubbard, who seem to remain behind in the utility corridor and hallways of Alcatraz.

JOHN ANGLIN (AZ1476), CLARENCE ANGLIN (AZ1485), FRANK MORRIS (AZ1441), ALLEN WEST (AZ1335)

June 11, 1962: Most people think that Frank Morris was the mastermind behind the spectacular escape from Alcatraz in 1962. But Clarence Carnes, the youngest inmate to be sent to Alcatraz and co-conspirator in the Battle of Alcatraz escape attempt, has publicly said that the plot originated with an inmate named Allen West.

West was assigned to paint the top tier and ceiling of the cellblock. While doing this job, he realized that it would be relatively easy to make it to the roof of the building through the ventilation shaft. The ducts were constructed with metal crossbars, but if the entire duct was cut from its surrounding support and shoved outward, it was then easy to make it to the roof.

West approached brothers Clarence and John Anglin—both doing time for bank robbery and both of whom had a history of escape from other prisons—and asked if they would like to partner up with him. The Anglins agreed but wanted to bring their friend Frank Morris into the plot as well. They told West that Morris would be a great asset due to his ability to think on the move. Philip Bergan, former captain of the guards at Alcatraz, said of Morris, "He was a thinker. Anything connected with this escape that had any brains behind it can be credited to Morris."

Carnes had told Morris about the utility corridors they had found during the earlier escape attempt and said that the pipes in the corridor could be used as a makeshift ladder all the way up to the ventilation shaft. Morris, testing the back wall of his cell, found that it could be dug through around the ventilation ducts and made wide enough so as to reach the utility corridor directly behind the cell. So every day during "music hour," that time of the evening when inmates and guards would get together and play their musical instruments, the four convicts worked on the walls. Using stolen spoons from the mess and an improvised drill, they diligently and patiently worked on their plan.

At the same time that the four men picked away at their cell walls, they were also gathering in the pieces of the puzzle that were needed to construct a makeshift raft and life preservers: fifty raincoats, some stolen, some given by other inmates who were let in on the plan. Using the raincoats, each escapee made his own life preserver. Morris and the Anglin brothers then used the remainder of the coats to assemble a raft they could use to get off the island. Growing up in Florida, Clarence and John Anglin had become expert raftsmen while fishing and exploring the swamps and the Everglades. They not only knew how to construct a raft, they also knew how to use currents, something that would be greatly needed while negotiating the waters of San Francisco Bay. At night, when lights out was called, the conspirators hid the raft and preservers in the openings they had made in the cell walls.

One of the problems that the convicts needed to overcome was being found out too soon to make a clean getaway. Morris came up with the

It was a ventilation grate just like this one that Morris and the Anglin brothers chipped away at to facilitate their escape.

brilliant idea of constructing dummy heads that could pass for each one of the inmates. At night, during rounds, the lights were dimmed down and the guards would casually walk the blocks making sure each prisoner was in bed. All Morris and the others had to do is make something close enough to fool the guards in the low light conditions. The Anglin brothers started fabricating dummy heads out of homemade cement, toilet paper and soap.

Frank Morris's cell on Alcatraz, complete with his fabricated head.

The fake heads were crude but lifelike. While the brothers were making the heads, Morris approached Leon "Whitey" Thompson to ask him if he would mix up some flesh-tone coloring. Thompson was an artist who had been doing a lot of oil painting on Alcatraz. Thompson was the right person to ask and even created what the inmates needed to get the faces just the right tone to match each convict. To make them even more lifelike, the Anglins, who worked in the prison barbershop, brought human hair back to their cells at the end of the day and pasted it onto the four dummy heads.

The last obstacle to their plan was how to inflate their homemade raft. They knew that they didn't have time or the wherewithal to blow the raft up by themselves, but they didn't have anything that they could bring with them to do it any other way. Frank Morris came up with a brilliant idea using an item small enough to carry with them and easy enough to use that it would only require a short amount of time to accomplish the task. Morris had been given a small accordion known as a concertina that he used during music hour. By removing the keys and using the instrument as a bellows, he was able to fill the raft.

It took the conspirators eight months to drill out the ventilation shaft and collect the things they would need to get off the island. They also had to build a raft, dummy heads, life preservers and fake vent covers to put over their cell vents to keep the guards from seeing what they were doing. It took patience and determination that had been lacking in every other escape attempt in the past. In his memoirs, Clarence Carnes wrote, "Many times through the years I'd met men who had tried to escape. But their flaw had been too little planning and being too hasty. They had not been thorough in their thinking and that's what defeated them. But not this time."

On the night that the conspirators chose for their escape, the prisoners slipped out of their cells through the small holes they had chiseled around the air vents and gathered up the items that had been stashed in the corridor. When Allen West failed to appear from his cell, Frank Morris went to see if there was a problem and found West trying to squeeze through the hole. West had misjudged the size of the hole he had dug and was unable to fit through into the utility corridor. The others couldn't wait for him to resolve the situation and left him behind. (The following day, the guards found West sleeping soundly in his bed.)

The Anglins and Morris climbed up the heating pipes to the ceiling, removed the ventilation ducts they had previously cut during the last eight months and made their way onto the roof. Dashing one hundred feet across the prison roof, the three convicts found a pipe leading down to the ground next to the shower area. Carrying the equipment they had made, they carefully made their way down the side of the cell house and ran for the waters of the bay. No one knows what happened to Frank Morris or the Anglin brothers once they entered into the cold North Bay waters, but Allen West said that the plan was to make it to Angel Island, rest and then swim through Raccoon Straits and into Marin. Once there, they would steal a car, break into a clothing store and then go their separate ways. That was the plan at least. The FBI, of course, thinks something completely different.

This pipe allowed Morris and the Anglins to get off the roof of the cellblock.

The dummy heads that the inmates had created worked exactly like planned. Every time one of the guards passed by, they saw the heads with their tufts of hair sticking out of the blankets and assumed that the prisoners were asleep and secure. Once the deception was discovered and the prisoners found missing, one of the largest manhunts ever ensued. In the first day of the search, no clue about the whereabouts of the escapees was found. Then, bits and pieces of evidence started turning up. One of the homemade oars they had used for paddling was found floating between Angel Island and Alcatraz, and then a piece of the raft itself. A day after finding these pieces of the escape, a small, watertight bag was found; inside was an address book, some photographs and a money order. The photos and money order showed that these belonged to the Anglin brothers. Then, the Norwegian freighter *Norefjell* reported a body floating in the water outside the Golden Gate Bridge. The description the Norwegian captain gave of the body they had seen seemed to match that of Frank Morris. After months of investigations turned up nothing else, the FBI concluded that the three men had drowned in their attempt. Officially, Clarence and John Anglin and Frank Morris are listed as "missing, presumed dead."

This photo shows the roof near where the Anglins and Morris made their way to the ground. Notice the placement of the guard position.

The dummy head of John Anglin.

In a twist on this case, a day after the escape, a man called a San Francisco law office known to represent Alcatraz prisoners and identified himself as John Anglin. The man wanted the clerk to call the U.S. marshal's office. When the clerk refused, the caller asked if she knew who he was and if not to turn on the news. The man then hung up the phone. Inmate Clarence Carnes said that a few weeks after the escape, he received a postcard that simply said, "Gone Fishing." According to Carnes and other inmates, this was a code phrase to let the other inmate know they had succeeded in their escape.

In 2013, a letter was sent to the San Francisco Police Department from someone claiming to be John Anglin. This letter forced the agency to reopen the case into the escape. The letter said, "My name is John Anglin. I escaped from Alcatraz in June 1962 with my brother Clarence and Frank Morris. I am 83 years old and in bad shape. I have cancer. Yes, we all made it that night but barely!"

The Anglin family has received several letters since, and some pictures have even surfaced, said to be of both John and Clarence Anglin, taken long after the 1962 attempt. There is plenty of evidence to support whichever theory one wants to gravitate toward, and the unknown quantity of each still adds a layer of mystery to either one. It is up to the reader which one is to be believed.

Author's note: It has recently come to light that even though the FBI claimed to have never found the raft used by the Anglins and Morris or that no sign of the three has ever been found, that might not actually be the truth. Documents released under the FOIA laws show that the raft was recovered on Angel Island and that a report was filed of three men matching the description of the escapees stealing a 1955 blue Chevrolet in Marin the same day as the escape.

CHAPTER 6
HISTORIC GHOSTS OF "THE ROCK"

Alcatraz is known as the most feared prison in America's history. It is known as an inescapable fortress that drove men insane. It is known as the most visited tourist attraction in San Francisco. It is known as "the Rock." It is also known as one of the most haunted places in the United States, and for good reason.

The island has a long and storied reputation for having supernatural phenomena occur on its shores. The early Native Americans (Bay Miwok or Ohlone) living in and around the bay thought the island was home to evil spirits. If a member broke tribal law, he would be sent to the island as punishment; if the crime was severe enough, he could be banished there for life. The Ohlone believed that Alcatraz was a gathering place for these evil spirits, and their lore states that the atmosphere there is "heavy and depressing." It was well known among the tribe that anyone sentenced to punishment on the island was more likely than not to go completely insane.

Over the years, archaeologists have excavated areas of Alcatraz and have found numerous human bone fragments. Since the island never knew a burial while under the control of the United States, it is logical to believe that even though the island was feared by the Miwok, they also used Alcatraz as a burial site. It is not known, however, if the bones found here are of those who died on the mainland or are those who were sentenced to languish and die on the island itself.

The Ohlone would hold rituals on the island as a way to appease the spirits in the hopes that they would have prosperity and healthy crops, but the fog

A block is the oldest section of the prison. It still contains some of the original stairways the army installed.

around Alcatraz would come up thick, fast and unexpectedly, and many of the Miwok would die while trying to find their way both on the shore and in their boats. These deaths could account for the many reports from former guards and prisoners of hearing screams along the water's edge, seeing what appears to be Native American dances that are accompanied by the staccato beat of drums and hearing voices chanting out in song. These visions have only been fleeting, and many believed that they were nothing more than the prisoners' growing insanity from isolation or the guards' loneliness while stationed on the Rock. However, as more and more reports of this activity have surfaced over the years, it is becoming accepted as what some think it may be: the spirits of the Ohlone keeping the evil at bay.

Today, staff and visitors alike can still hear the sounds of phantom whistles, screams and men's voices calling out in fear. Many of the terrified screams of pain and wailing come from one end of A block, that section of the original fortress now known as "the Dungeon."

THE DUNGEON

This section of the prison was once known as the Citadel and was the original fortress complex for the defense of the island. In 1909, the army began taking apart the old fortress but left the bottom floor to act as the basement for the new cell house that was planned for the site. The old ammo magazines and other rooms were used for storage, with a few of them being put aside for punishment cells for the more unruly prisoners, while the moat became an outer passageway that ran around the outer part of the basement. When the army gave Alcatraz over to the Bureau of Prisons in 1934, these areas were still there underneath the new federal penitentiary. Warden Johnston decided that this area would be the perfect place to punish the prisoners now under his care who broke any of the rules he had put in place.

Most prisoners who entered the "Dungeon," as the basement was now being called, never wanted to go back. So bad was the treatment and so uncomfortable the accommodations that some even went mad while serving time there. The entire ward was pitch black once the guards left and closed the door, the floor was constantly wet from the dripping cisterns and the sounds of rats running around the floors and walls were a constant reminder to the inmates that they could be bitten—or worse—at any moment. If a prisoner could actually sleep, it had to be done while sitting against a wall or lying in the water on the floor. The guards would come down several times a day and at night to wake those who had managed to find sleep, and they were fed a diet of mostly bread and water. They were supposed to get a hot meal of soup every three days, but the guards often ignored even this meager nicety. If the guards were really in a mean mood, they would put the inmate "on the water." This unkind act had the guard throwing a bucket of cold water on the prisoner and letting him shiver until he finally dried off, which, considering the cold and damp conditions in the Dungeon, could take hours.

Federal law allowed an inmate to spend only nineteen days in any punishment confinement, but there are records that show prisoners spent much longer than that in the Dungeon at Alcatraz. In the movie *Murder in the First*, starring Kevin Bacon, inmate Joe Bowers is portrayed having spent months in the cold, wet and dark lower underbelly of the prison. Others, such as James Grove, came out of the Dungeon insane, although there is evidence that he might have been that way when originally confined. It wasn't until 1935 that James Bennett, director of the Bureau of Prisons, began looking into the solitary confinement practices at Alcatraz. That was the year that inmate John Standig committed suicide after he spent ten days in the dungeon for an escape attempt. Even though the findings showed that the Dungeon was "cruel and unusual punishment," it still took until 1942 to completely abandon the basement and come up with an alternate solitary confinement cell.

Today, both visitors and rangers alike report strange things in and around the Dungeon below cellblock A. Tourists regularly approach the rangers who work in the cell house with reports of hearing men calling up from the basement. At first, these reports were taken to heart, and the basement would be searched for anyone who might have wandered down the circular staircase and gotten lost in the maze of rooms and alcoves in the Dungeon. No one was ever found. Over the years, those working at Alcatraz came to the realization that what these visitors were hearing must be spirits, although officially the park service disputes all reports of ghosts, even the ones the rangers have begun to believe.

One ranger working in the late afternoon heard screams coming from the Dungeon. Thinking it was a tourist who had become lost from their group, she hurried down the spiral staircase and followed the screaming in what she called a "game of hide-and-seek." The ranger never found anyone, and for a long time she didn't report the incident out of fear that her co-workers would make fun of her for following what she now believed was a ghost from the prison's past. It took a few months of soul searching, but the ranger finally came clean on what had happened to her that evening, and when she told her supervisor and fellow rangers, she was surprised that most of them had similar experiences with the cold and dark passageways of the Dungeon.

Even the steadfast, no-nonsense Warden Johnston, who did not believe in ghosts in the least, had an event happen to him while giving a tour of the prison to a number of guests that he couldn't explain. Johnston had a group of federal prison officials touring their newest maximum-security lockup, and he wanted to familiarize his guests with the cellblocks. While showing them around A block and the old "dungeons" below, a strange, eerie wail began to emanate from the basement below them. It was quiet at first, but as they stood there, the sounds of sobbing got louder. Everyone in the group could hear what was now the unmistakable sound of a woman crying. Even the warden was forced to admit that it was coming from the Dungeon area, which was now off-limits to most personnel. As the group listened, they began to comment on how the sobbing seemed to be coming from the walls of the prison and not just echoing off them. It was almost as if the prison itself was weeping. The group stood for a few minutes more listening to pitiful sobbing and then turned to go; as they headed out of the cellblock, the wailing suddenly stopped, and it is said that a gust of icy cold wind swept over the group, as if telling them goodbye.

This event shook Warden Johnston, and he never could explain what had occurred. He didn't like to talk about what had happened, but he wasn't finished with the ghosts of Alcatraz. Johnston would again come face to face with the unknown, but this time it would be in his own home.

THE WARDEN'S MANSION

The Hoe House, more commonly referred to as the warden's mansion, was one of those places that stood out among the sparse, utilitarian buildings of the federal penitentiary. Alcatraz was never designed for more than the most basic of comforts, let alone the luxurious appointments provided the master of the island. This three-story, seventeen-room mansion, built in 1921 (some say 1929), was the site of many elaborate and grandiose parties through the years the prison was in operation. All four of the wardens of Alcatraz found the accommodations more suited to the wealthy elite than the public servants that they were, yet of course, none of them ever complained.

One can just make out the still standing warden's mansion (Hoe House). Just a few days after this photo was taken, the Hoe House would be destroyed by fire.

All the occupants of the mansion used the more cooperative and docile prisoners as their domestic help, and these prisoners found that these jobs were some of the easiest and safest within the penitentiary. The work was not rigorous. House cleaning, scrubbing, helping with the cooking and acting as butlers, servers and valets were a far cry from the work done in the prison itself. Even when the stories of ghosts within the mansion began to circulate among the inmates, who were always a superstitious lot, they still vied for the jobs within the house.

One of the first reports of apparitions within the home came one night just before Christmas. Warden Johnston was throwing one of his famous Christmas parties, and while the festivities were in full swing, with guards lining the walls to keep an eye on the inmate help, the entire party came to an abrupt halt. The reason everyone in the room suddenly stopped the celebrations had to do with an unexpected and completely unknown party crasher appearing out of nowhere in front of the startled group, the warden included. The man in front of them wore a gray suit and a hat with a full brim and sported a handsome set of muttonchop sideburns. What they noticed most, however, was that the man was transparent. The specter looked around the room for a moment and seemed to sigh, and then an icy cold swept over the entire room. Being Christmas in San Francisco, the island was already freezing cold. The room had a very large Benjamin Franklin stove that had a raging fire going inside to keep the room warm, but the icy cold brought on by the ghost was so bitter that the stove was instantly extinguished. Almost as if the now unlit fireplace had been his cue, the spirit vanished, leaving the warden and his guests wondering just what, or who, they had witnessed.

A few years after the event at the Christmas party, some officers and guards of the prison were enjoying a relaxing night playing poker in the mansion's game room. Sometime around midnight, the men looked up from their game to see the same spirit from the night of the Christmas party watching their poker match. This time, however, the ghost was reported to be wearing a dark, double-breasted suit and a dark brimmed hat. The specter still wore his distinctive muttonchop sideburns, which is how the group knew it was the same ghost. As before, the spirit stood watching the men for a few moments and then, with the same blast of icy cold air, he vanished from sight.

The warden's mansion today is nothing but a shell of its former self. In June 1970, during the height of the Native American occupation of Alcatraz, a fire swept through the building, destroying everything in its path. The once grand home all but collapsed, leaving nothing but the outside walls intact. During the 1980s, the remaining structure almost collapsed but was saved from complete ruin by a combination of Hollywood money (a studio wanted to use the island in a feature film) and National Parks determination. The condition of the old mansion, however, seems not to have bothered the ghosts of the building, or they might not have even noticed that the house is no longer complete.

The warden's mansion as it sits today, a victim of carelessness or deliberate malice.

Rangers patrolling Alcatraz at night have reported seeing strange lights moving about the ruins. These lights linger in what was once the parlor of the house, and there has been more than one light gathered at a time. Some of the rangers have said it looks almost as if the lights are gathered for a party. Other reports from the rangers include hearing whispered conversations as they pass by the front of the structure, and on occasion, the mutton-chopped man has been seen briefly standing in various "rooms" of the house.

Tourists have reported seeing wisps of fog on an otherwise clear day move through the building only to vanish as quickly as they appeared, and others have reported hearing the sound of laughter coming from the now gutted interior. One visitor to the prison even reported to a ranger that a "tourist" had gone into the house past the "keep out" signs. When the ranger and the guest arrived back at the mansion, no one was found inside, nor could they find anyone who matched the description given anywhere on the island.

It is sad that this beautiful structure is now destroyed by the careless acts of those with no thought for the history of others. The ghosts don't seem to have noticed what has transpired in this building, and it seems they are also unaware that the structure next to the old Hoe House is no longer that which they knew in life.

THE ALCATRAZ LIGHTHOUSE

The original foundation for the first lighthouse on Alcatraz was laid down in January 1853, with the structure itself completed in July of that same year. The light would not be lit for another year due to the delay in obtaining the new Fresnel lens that had been ordered. The original structure was a one-and-a-half-story wooden cottage with the light tower protruding up from the center of the roof.

The first head light keeper was Michael Kassin, and his assistant was John Sloan; later, a second assistant was added. The head light keeper was given the use of four rooms, while each assistant was given two, and all three shared the kitchen. This lighthouse was built at the same time that the first Citadel was being constructed, and these fortifications were completed in 1859 just north of the beacon on the uppermost plateau of Alcatraz.

When the 1906 San Francisco earthquake struck at 5:30 a.m. on April 18, the head light keeper, Henry Young, wrote in the log, "Violent and continuous earthquake....San Francisco on fire....Is this the end of the

The "new" lighthouse constructed to replace the old wooden structure.

world? Terrible seeing S.F. from here." The damage to the lighthouse tower was relatively minor. The light would revolve for only three more years, however, because in 1909, the old Citadel was razed and the new cell house, being much taller, interfered with the beacon's operation. New plans were drawn up for a ninety-foot-tall, reinforced concrete tower to be built just south of the original lighthouse, replete with comfortable housing in two two-story wings for the keeper and his two assistants.

Even though the old lighthouse and building were demolished after the new tower opened, that would not be the end of the story for the former guardian of the bay. Almost from the first day after the old light was gone from existence, reports began to filter in of it reappearing on foggy nights. No one is really clear why the house and beacon return, but so many stories have come about that it is clear something is being seen that shouldn't be there. One guard from the 1940s said that he had been walking his rounds in the early hours of an extremely foggy morning when he heard the sound of moaning coming from the area between the prison and the light tower and headed in that direction. When he neared the area where the sound was coming from, he saw something begin to shimmer directly in front of him, and a building appeared to materialize where he was standing. The guard said that he stumbled backward to get out of the way as an old-style lighthouse came into existence, complete with rotating beacon light and foghorn. The guard quit the following day.

No one knows why the lighthouse keeps reappearing, but over the years, those who have seen the spectral building said that before the old lighthouse comes into view, an eerie whistling sound will be heard and a strange, flashing green light will slowly circle around the island. The lighthouse will always vanish as quickly as it appears, leaving the viewer to wonder if it had only been their imagination at work or truly a ghostly visage.

THE LAUNDRY ROOM

The laundry room on Alcatraz has had so many reports over the years that many people claim it is the most haunted area of the island. Guards, guides, rangers and guests alike have all reported the same things. The smell of smoke will become so overwhelming that it is believed a fire has broken out in the building. People will sometimes be evacuated from the area, but when crews go to inspect the room where they think the fire and smoke is emanating from, there is no sign of any fire, smoke or damage. The smell of smoke also disappears. This has been reported so often that it has become an urban legend attached to the island.

The closest thing to a C block laundry room is the laundry distribution center below the cellblock next to the showers.

One of the things that is strange about these stories is that the laundry facilities were actually in the building dubbed the Model Industries Building. This structure on the northeast corner of the island was used until 1939, when a new building was built. The new structure had its entire upper floor devoted to laundry and dry cleaning. There never was a C block laundry room.

Another strange urban legend that has grown up around the laundry room ghosts is that of Abie "Butcher" Maldowitz. A renowned psychic is the one who picked up on the Butcher and said that he was killed in the C block laundry room by two other inmates. This story has been passed down in print, media and lore ever since. Books, newspapers and magazines have claimed, "Prison records show that Maldowitz was killed…" Unfortunately, what prison records show is that at no time in the history of the prison was there ever an inmate by that name or nickname.

One can only wonder how a story with no basis in fact can become one of the most famous ghost tales from a prison whose records are open for anyone to see or why no fact-check was ever done, but the story is one of the creepier tales that have sprung up around the island.

THE MODEL INDUSTRIES BUILDING

This building on the northwest corner of the island has seen so much violence and death that it should come as no surprise that it is haunted. From Officer Cline being beaten to death with a hammer in 1938 to Henri Young stabbing Rufus McCain in 1941, this part of the island is a magnet for reports of spirit sightings.

The building itself has seen better days and is not usually on the more established tour routes, but over the years, tourists and guards have reported seeing the apparition of a guard slowly making his rounds of the building. The spirit is seen looking around, sometimes carrying a billy club and always alert. This guard will glance in the direction of the living but gives them a look of suspicion, as if he sees them as inmates rather than visitors or guests. If the specter is approached, he will simply shake his head and vanish from view. The rangers and employees working at Alcatraz today believe this may be the ghost of Officer Royal Cline, the guard who was brutally killed with a hammer during the escape attempt by Limerick, Lucas and Franklin.

This tunnel travels for a few hundred feet and terminates at the Model Industries Building. This and other tunnels constructed by the military gave rise to the "secret" tunnels of Alcatraz legends.

Another spirit that is seen here could be that of Rufus McCain. When Henri Young stabbed McCain with his homemade shiv, he didn't kill him outright. McCain was taken to the hospital ward and there suffered in extreme pain from a gut wound before he succumbed to his injuries. All those who were there at the time said that the pain the man felt while dying was excruciating, and watching McCain slip in and out of consciousness was hard for them. Even though he was a hardened criminal, no one should have to go through that much agony, or so they said.

The reports from guests and employees alike all say the same thing. A man in a prisoner's uniform is seen running through the building. Before he can reach the safety of a door or hallway, the specter will suddenly stop, clutch his stomach and then fade from view as he falls to the floor. On rare occasions, the person relating the story has said that blood can be seen spurting out of a wound. If this specter is indeed McCain, this is not the only place he is haunting. It is said that the red-eyed monster that dwells in D block may in fact be none other than Rufus McCain seeking his revenge for his horrible death.

CELL 14D

This cell in D block where co-author Bob Davis experienced his first paranormal occurrence is arguably the most notorious place in the most notorious prison in America. So many people have had things happen to them in this spot over the years that the National Park Service has now had the doors welded open on all five of the "hole" cells. At one time, these cells were used to let tourists get an idea of what it must have been like to be locked into a lightless cell with a double set of doors, one solid and soundproof, one barred. The rangers would let volunteers enter one of the cells, usually 14D, and then shut the door. Even though the door was unlocked and the guest could faintly hear the other people talking on the outside, many times this seemingly harmless scenario would end with the tourist screaming in terror to be let out of the cell.

D block was the segregation unit in Alcatraz. Only the most violent, most incorrigible prisoners were housed here. Privileges, as scarce as they were on the Rock, were even less for the inmates in cellblock D. Robert Stroud, before being transferred to the medical ward for illnesses, had his permanent cell on this block. The rule of silence that the inmates had to endure in the early days of the prison was enforced much more stringently here, as were the rest of the rules. The inmates in the general population knew that a transfer to D block meant spending even harder time than they currently were serving. As bad as D block could be, the five cells in D block that were solitary confinement were much worse.

Five cells on the lower level of D block, or as it was called on the island, the Treatment Unit were set aside for solitary confinement. These punishment cells for those already in the punishment block could only be opened by guards in the gun gallery, and the single light in these cells could only be turned off and on by the guards, not the prisoner occupying the cell. Each unit had two doors: one inner door that was like any other in the prison and an outer soundproof solid metal door. Once closed, this outer door allowed no light to enter the cell. Inmates in these cells were not allowed to eat with the other prisoners but had their food brought to them and had to eat alone. Each prisoner put into a dark cell was given one pair of socks, shorts and coveralls—not enough to keep the inmate warm inside a metal box on the windward side of the cold San Francisco Bay. They were fed the same meals as the other convicts, but if they were found to be uncooperative or unruly, their food would be mashed together in an unappetizing glob of mush. Each one of these cells contained a toilet, a sink and a metal bed frame. The mattress was taken away each morning and given back only at lights out. These five cells became known as "dark cells."

The fifth solitary confinement cell was reserved for the worst of the worst. Only inmates who had committed infractions of a violent or horrendous act against other prisoners would be placed in this cell. Inmates who had harmed another prisoner or guard while trying to escape were also put into this cell as punishment. This last cell had none of the furnishings of the dark cells, a hole in the floor that could only be flushed by the guards, no sink and no bed or mattress. This cell became known as the "strip cell." The cell number was 14D.

Almost every inmate was scared of being placed inside one of the dark cells. They were terrified of 14D. Their fear of the strip cell had little to do with the condition of the cell or the discomfort they knew would accompany a stay and all that would entail. All of that could be overlooked. What terrified the inmates were the stories of the red-eyed demon that inhabited the cell.

Shortly after D block was built and opened in 1940, reports started coming in about spirits inhabiting the solitary confinement section. Even though each one of the dark cells seemed to have a spirit, it was the strip

The most notorious cell on Alcatraz: the infamous 14D.

cell that had the reputation as being the home of a killer ghost. The tale is still widely told today.

The story goes that sometime in the mid-1940s, an inmate was put into cell 14D and a short time later began calling for the guards to let him out. He said that there was someone in the cell with him and that the other person was going to kill him. The inmate kept pleading with the guards. As his voice rose to a scream and his pleas became mournful, the convict began saying that he could see the other inmate's eyes and that they were glowing red. He screamed that there was a demon in the cell with him.

The guards on duty that night figured that the man was just trying to get out of the dreaded strip cell and thought that this wild story would at the very least get him taken to the medical ward for evaluation. The guards had heard every story the inmates had ever tried to use and, as such, ignored the inmate's cries for help. Finally, the inmate quieted down. The guards figured he had gone to sleep, and they settled in for the night.

The next morning, as D block gathered for the morning prisoner count, the guards opened the strip cell and found the inmate dead. The prisoner had red marks around his throat, as if he had been strangled to death, and his face was twisted into a terrified expression. No one else was found in the cell, and the coroner confirmed the cause of death as strangulation. The report also went on to say that the death was not by suicide.

The following morning, as the prisoners stood in line for the head count, the guards counted one extra inmate. As they were performing the recount, they realized that the prisoner who had died the previous day was standing in line. As the stunned guards and terrified prisoners watched, the dead convict faded out of sight.

Unfortunately, there is no record of an inmate dying in cell 14D nor any record of a prisoner dying in this fashion. The tale itself seems to be one of those urban legends that have sprung up out of the haunted reputation of Alcatraz. That is not to say that 14D is not occupied by at least one spirit. There are plenty of stories surrounding this cell from both employees of Alcatraz and tourists alike. The theory that is most widely disseminated is that Rufus McCain, due to his long incarceration within the cell, is the spirit causing all of the havoc in the strip cell.

As is told in another section of this book, co-author Bob Davis had a surprisingly similar thing happen when he was shut into the cell, but Bob is not the only one who has had a frightening experience within the cell since the prison opened up as a tourist attraction.

Although not spacious by any sense of the word, a regular cell on Alcatraz was opulent compared to the "strip cell," 14D.

In the late 1980s, a tourist complained to a docent at the prison that she had been inside the cell and the door had mysteriously shut. She couldn't get it open and began banging on the door and calling for help. She said that just before the door opened, she was groped. She could clearly feel someone fondling her. As soon as the door swung open, the touching ceased, and she realized that there was no one in the cell with her.

Who or what is haunting the strip cell may never be known, and some of the stories that have been passed down are now under severe scrutiny due to our Internet culture. The one thing that most can agree on regarding this section of the prison is that it appears to be one of the most haunted areas on the island of Alcatraz.

CHAPTER 7
GHOSTS OF FAMOUS INMATES

No one really knows why a person haunts a location. What is even more unusual and odd for those of us who wonder about such things is why a person would haunt an area that they despised, feared or were desperate to get away from. Whatever the reason may be, Alcatraz seems to have not only caught the imagination of people from all over the world but has also caught, and held, the imagination and spirits of those who once were held captive on the island. Some of the most violent and desperate men ever to live in this country and who wanted nothing more than to escape the rigors of being a prisoner on the island have, for one reason or another, found themselves still trapped on Alcatraz after death has claimed them.

ROBERT "THE BIRDMAN" STROUD (AZ594)

Many people have heard about the "Birdman of Alcatraz." Most, however, have no idea who he was or that he was never allowed to have birds while doing time on the Rock. Many don't even know his name was Robert Stroud. Others only know him as the benevolent, peaceful inmate portrayed by Burt Lancaster. Robert Stroud was anything but peaceful and benevolent.

Stroud was born in 1890 in Seattle, Washington, into a family that had an abusive, alcoholic father. By the time he was thirteen years old, Stroud had enough of the beatings and ran away from home, settling in Alaska. By the time he was eighteen years old, he had become a pimp, and he committed his first violent crime at the age of nineteen. A local bartender refused to pay one of his prostitutes, and Stroud shot him to death and took the man's wallet. Stroud was convicted of manslaughter and sentenced to twelve years.

While doing time at McNeil Island Penitentiary, Stroud was constantly getting into trouble. He would fight with other inmates, refuse commands from the guards and explode into fits of rage when challenged, going so far as to stab a fellow inmate. Stroud would steal narcotics by intimidating orderlies and pharmacy workers and once viciously attacked a hospital orderly for reporting him to prison authorities. The orderly spent time in the hospital due to the attack. The assault added six months to Stroud's sentence. Shortly afterward, he was transferred to Leavenworth Penitentiary.

Things didn't get any better while Stroud was finishing his sentence after the transfer. In 1916, his brother came to visit Stroud, but because of his unruly behavior, the visitation was denied. Stroud again went into a rage and this time, in front of 1,100 other inmates gathered in the mess hall, stabbed a guard to death. Robert Stroud was charged with first-degree murder and was sentenced to death by hanging. In a desperate plea to save her son's life, Stroud's mother convinced President Woodrow Wilson to commute his sentence to life in prison without parole. After this new ruling and because of his violent tendencies, Warden T.W. Morgan sent Stroud into the segregation unit, where he would live out his sentence in complete solitude.

Robert Stroud may have been segregated from the other convicts, but it was still required that he be allowed fresh air and daily trips to the recreation yard. It was during his yard time that he found an injured canary. Stroud took the bird back to his cell and nursed it back to health. From that moment on, Robert Stroud became fascinated with birds. Over the next thirty years, he would study every aspect of ornithology. He was even allowed to breed and keep birds in some of the isolation cells to raise and study. The warden deemed this a "productive use of his time." Stroud became so knowledgeable about canaries that he penned two books, *Diseases of Canaries* and *Stroud's Digest on the Diseases of Birds*. These books garnered him the respect of many of the world's greatest ornithologists of the time. Stroud was given special equipment for his scientific studies; however, it was discovered that he was using some of this equipment as a still for homemade alcohol. Due to this, in 1942 he was transferred to Alcatraz. His time studying and keeping birds was at an end.

It was here, in these medical ward cells, that Robert "Birdman" Stroud spent most of his time on Alcatraz.

Stroud spent the first six years of his time on Alcatraz in D block. That section was known as the "hole" and was the segregation ward for the prison. Stroud did have limited contact with other inmates, something he lacked while at Leavenworth. Without the distractions of his birds, Stroud began studying law and penned two more books: *Bobbie*, an autobiography, and *Looking Outward: The U.S. Prison System from Colonial Times to the Formation of the Bureau of Prisons*. Neither of these titles was allowed to be published until after his death.

The climate at Alcatraz was not good for Stroud, who had always been rather sickly. After six years of the cold and damp weather of San Francisco, Robert Stroud was transferred to a cell in the prison hospital ward. He would spend the next eleven years there suffering from ailments these weather conditions brought on. By 1959, his health was failing, and he was transferred for the final time. Stroud was moved to the Medical Center for Federal Prisoners in Springfield, Missouri. Robert Stroud died of natural causes on November 21, 1963.

The Birdman didn't pass away at Alcatraz, and his inability to study or keep his beloved canaries made the prison a miserable place for Stroud to spend time. No one can say why a person would come back to haunt a location that was detested as much as Stroud hated the Rock, but if reports are to be believed, that is exactly what he is doing.

His upstairs cell in D block has a history of guests seeing a full-body apparition standing outside the cell and staring down at tourists as if studying them. The tales say that the man is wearing a prison uniform, and some have even claimed to have seen the number 594 printed across the breast of the shirt. This inmate number is that of Robert Stroud. Tour guides and rangers have also reported seeing Stroud. Most of the time, the specter only glares at those in uniform with a menacing stare, and on occasion, the spirit will slowly shake his head and vanish from sight as the stunned employee watches.

Another area where Robert Stroud is seen and heard is the room in the medical ward where he spent eleven years. This area of Alcatraz has been closed off to the public for quite a few years due to its poor condition. However, night tours are led through the medical ward, and on occasion, those lucky enough to be spending the entire night on the island are allowed to walk through this area. Many, many reports from the medical ward room where Stroud spent most of his time claim to hear the sound of cards being shuffled or hushed talking that stops as soon as anyone nears the cell. Stroud was allowed to play cards and chess with those guards who were willing, and it is believed that it is the residual sound of these games that is being reported.

Reports of seeing a man pacing the large cell room in the medical ward have also been made, mostly from those wandering the area late at night or in the early morning hours. This apparition appears not to notice witnesses but will always fade from view before anyone can get too close.

People have also told of hearing the sound of birds coming from both his D block cell as well as the medical ward cell. As the Birdman was not allowed to keep his canaries here, we believe these reports are most likely the result of either an overactive imagination or the person's desire to find the infamous inmate while on Alcatraz.

Robert Stroud never got to view the movie that was supposedly his life story behind bars. However, shortly before he died, Stroud was able to meet Burt Lancaster and speak with him for a short while. Lancaster would go on to win the Best Actor Oscar for his performance, but in so doing, he did a great disservice to the public in his portrayal of Robert Stroud as a benevolent and misunderstood criminal. Stroud was a vicious murderer with a long list of violent offenses. In essence, Stroud was as close to a monster as an ordinary human can be. It is sad that this man has been given a legacy through books and film that he does not deserve.

GHOSTS OF THE BATTLE OF ALCATRAZ

The Battle of Alcatraz was one of those escape attempts that couldn't have gone worse. From the very start, Cretzer, Coy and Hubbard should have realized that whatever it was they had planned was never going to work and that surrender was their only option. If they had been smart, they would have only had some time added to their sentences. The three men were not smart, and it ended up costing them their lives instead.

The battle itself was explained in an earlier chapter and we won't revisit it here, but what we want to let people know is what effects the aftermath of this escape attempt might have had on those involved. Hubbard, Cretzer and Coy may have paid the ultimate price for their crimes, but it appears they may be paying that price far longer than they deserve. It seems that the three cohorts are destined to walk the corridors of Alcatraz in death as they did in life.

The utility corridor between where the three inmates met their untimely and violent death is said to still be haunted by the three. One of the most famous stories surrounding this event is from an employee who was stationed on the island to guard against intruders. The watchman was near C block when he began hearing strange noises coming from the utility corridor between C and B blocks. It was in 1976, and the Native American takeover of Alcatraz was still fresh in his mind, so when he heard bangs and clanging coming from the corridor, he thought it might be a prowler sneaking about. The watchman went to the door where Cretzer, Coy and Hubbard had been killed, stood there for a minute and realized the noises were coming from inside the utility corridor. The man opened the door, and the sounds immediately stopped. The watchman, shining his flashlight down through the pipes of the corridor, couldn't see a thing; there was no one in the utility hallway. The man closed the door and walked away.

As the night watchman walked away down the cellblock, the clangs and bangs started up again. This time they seemed louder. He quickly made his way back to the door and opened it once again. There was still nothing inside the utility corridor that wasn't supposed to be there—still no person could be found. The man walked away once more, shaking his head and wondering if the noises were the reason that this door had once been welded shut.

Today, the utility corridor door has been removed and a solid piece of Plexiglas has been installed. Alcatraz claims it is so tourists can peer down the corridor where such a famous escape took place. One has to wonder if

This utility corridor is where people believe they hear and feel the death throes of Cretzer, Hubbard and Coy. Next to 14D, it is considered one of the most haunted spots in the prison.

it has anything to do with the fact that this area is now recognized as one of the most haunted spots in the prison.

Over the years since Alcatraz has been opened as a tourist attraction, reports from guests near this area have included hearing the same type of noises that the watchman heard and becoming very dizzy if they get too close to the Plexiglas. Other people have said that they get a deep sense of sadness and confusion when looking down into the corridor. Still others have felt panic and a need to leave the area. Could these people be feeling the panic and dread that Coy, Hubbard and Cretzer must have felt as the grenades were being dropped down to kill them?

THE GHOST OF ALVIN "CREEPY KARPIS" KARPOWICZ (INMATE #325)

For as much notoriety and fame as Al Capone sought while playing the role of a gangster with a heart, Alvin Karpowicz worked just as hard to try to remain in the shadows—to keep his name out of the newspapers and off of the air waves. Karpis once said, "I wanted the fortune, just not the fame.

If you're famous, that's when the cops come looking for you. I didn't want them looking for me."

Alvin Francis Karpowicz (originally spelled Karpavicz) was born on August 10, 1907, in Montreal, Canada. His Lithuanian immigrant parents moved the family to Topeka, Kansas, when Alvin was only two, and he began his life of crime at the young age of ten. That was the year Karpis (his last name was changed by a teacher so it could be pronounced more easily) began stealing things from the stores he would pass by in town, or he would run errands for the local prostitutes. When Arthur Witchy moved into Karpis's neighborhood in 1918, Alvin, in a state of awe at being friends with a "bigshot," as Karpis called him, began doing anything Witchy asked of him, including robbing a grocery store. For the next few years, Karpis and Witchy kept up with their crime spree until, in 1922, the Karpowicz family moved to Chicago.

The first time Karpis was arrested didn't have anything to do with robbery or theft of any sort. In 1925, Karpis was caught riding on the roof of a passing train and was sentenced to thirty days on a chain gang in Florida. This might have been his first arrest, but it was only the beginning of a life that would be spent more in prison than out.

Over the next couple of years, Karpis would be arrested for minor and not so minor offenses and sentenced to both hard and easy time. He even managed to escape once from the Kansas State Reformatory along with three other inmates. Alvin managed to elude the authorities for a year but was finally apprehended and sent back to the same place he had escaped from. It didn't take long before Karpis was removed from the reformatory and sent to the Kansas State Penitentiary. It was there that Karpis met Fred Barker.

Karpis was released in 1931. Almost immediately, he joined forces with Barker and began robbing shops all over the state. When Fred's brother Arthur "Doc" Barker was released from jail in 1932, he joined up with Karpis, and the three men began robbing banks, trains and payroll shipments. The trio gathered other gang members and together formed the Karpis-Barker gang. It was at this time that Alvin picked up the nickname "Creepy." This came from one of the gang members saying that Alvin's smile was "just creepy" when talking about the holdups and killings.

The gang began terrorizing towns all over the Midwest, robbing banks and killing people in the process. It wasn't until they began kidnapping, however, that the FBI really stepped up its manhunt for the outlaws.

Their first victim was William Hamm of Hamm's Brewery. The millionaire's family paid $100,000 for his release. Bolstered by the ease

"Creepy" Karpis enjoyed working in the mess hall. He would often be heard humming the Hamm's beer jingle to remind him of his kidnapping of the Hamm heir.

of their first kidnapping, the gang did it again, but this time they made a grave mistake in their choice of victim. Even though they made a staggering $200,000 off the kidnapping, their victim, banker Edward Bremer, had close ties with President Franklin Roosevelt. FDR was outraged that one of his friends could be treated this way and demanded the culprits be apprehended.

Ma and Fred Barker were gunned down in a shootout with the FBI in Florida, and Karpis was almost caught in Atlantic City shortly afterward. Karpis and cohort Harry Campbell managed to shoot their way past the feds, leaving Alvin's pregnant girlfriend behind after she was struck by a bullet in the arm. After his escape, Creepy managed one last heist, reminiscent of the tales from the old West. Karpis robbed a train in spectacular fashion outside Garrettsville, Ohio, which netted $27,000.

Karpis was finally arrested on May 1, 1936, in New Orleans. Unlike most of the other public enemies, Karpis gave up without a shot being fired. Alvin had seen John Dillinger and "Pretty Boy" Floyd and even his friends Ma and Fred Barker gunned down. He didn't want that happening to him. He was sentenced to life in prison and sent to Alcatraz, but he figured that was still better than being dead.

Alvin "Creepy" Karpis has the distinction of being the last public enemy no. 1 captured and being the longest-serving inmate ever to serve time on Alcatraz, from August 1936 to April 1962. Even though Karpis was released from jail and spent his last years of life in a small apartment in Spain, dying in 1979, perhaps his long duration incarcerated on the Rock is the reason that so many people today see his ghost wandering the island.

While on Alcatraz, Karpis had many jobs over the years, but one he seemed to enjoy the most was working in the kitchen and mess hall. Today, many tourists to the prison feel as if they are being watched when looking into the kitchen area through the bars erected to keep them from going inside. Figures will dart around in the back areas of the bakery, and guests have heard the distinct sound of pots and pans being moved; some even say they can hear someone washing the dishware. One guest swears he heard a man laughing right before the loud bang of a pot being thrown against the wall. Karpis was known as a troublemaker and liked to fight with other inmates. Could this be his temper flaring in the afterlife?

Other reports from the kitchen include the sounds of whistling and muted conversations. One tour guide even reported hearing his name

Alvin Karpis has been seen and heard haunting the kitchens on Alcatraz since his death in 1979.

being called out from the bakery even though he knew that no one could be in that section of the prison. People have said that on occasion they have heard the old Hamm's beer commercial being hummed or actually sung from the kitchens. It was well known among the inmates that Creepy Karpis would always chuckle whenever he heard the jingle come on while watching a baseball game on television. Many believe that what they are hearing is Karpis humming or singing this same tune and still laughing about his successful kidnapping.

Many wonder why Karpis would return to a place where he was locked up for so long. It might have something to do with his body being moved and then lost after he was evicted from his grave. When Alvin died, he was buried in a crypt in the local cemetery in Spain. The problem was that his estate only paid the rent on the crypt for a certain period of time. When that time ran out and no one came to pay for more, his remains were removed and interred in a mass unmarked pauper's grave. No one knows in which grave he was placed, and no records were ever filed.

The last public enemy no. 1, the prisoner who spent more time on Alcatraz than any other and the last bank robber to be captured before the end of the "golden age of organized crime" during the Depression years. For a gangster who never wanted the fame or notoriety, Alvin "Creepy" Karpis has become one of the most famous of his ilk.

THE GHOST OF AL "SCARFACE" CAPONE (AZ85)

You would be hard pressed to find anyone, even today, who has not heard of Al "Scarface" Capone, the notorious Chicago gangster who was pursued by the infamous Eliot "Untouchable" Ness. Capone has been immortalized in print, movies and even in song and seems to hold a special place in the consciousness of America itself. The stereotypical Hollywood gangster that Europeans think about when describing the tommy gun–toting American and the image that everyone has when the term "wise guy" is mentioned, all of this and more is embodied in the persona of Al Capone.

Alphonse Capone began his mob affiliation at age fifteen when he went to work for Johnny Torrio on the mean streets of Brooklyn, New York. Torrio would become one of Al's close friends and his mentor. Capone felt right at home as a bouncer in the gang's bars and brothels or as a part-time enforcer when needed. While working at a bar one night, Capone made a rude remark about the sister of local gangster Frank Galluccio, and Galluccio pulled out a knife or razor and slashed Capone's left cheek, leaving him with a deep scar. This gave Capone the enduring nickname of "Scarface."

Over the next decade, Torrio, after almost dying in an assassination attempt, retired, and Scarface took over the seat of power from his mentor. Capone ruled with an iron fist and a loaded temper. Outwardly, Capone came off as a benevolent businessman, and he himself never thought of himself as a gangster, criminal or crime lord. He always believed he was just a simple man of business, nothing more or less. Capone, unlike most other crime bosses of the time, didn't hide from the public eye; on the contrary, Al made a habit of getting out among the populace of Chicago. Always dressed in the finest suits, hats and finery of a proper gentleman, Capone took on the role of a respectable member of the community. He would give money out to friends and neighbors who were down on their luck, help out many in the community who needed it and revel in the attention he garnered and the cheers he received from the ballpark when he would attend games. Al Capone loved the limelight. He even once brokered a peace agreement between rival gangs when war seemed likely. His reputation grew to almost Robin Hood–like proportions. Capone always refused to carry a firearm as a sign of his status but never went anywhere without at least two heavily armed bodyguards.

Whoever Al Capone portrayed to the outside world, it was far removed from who he actually was in private. Scarface was a brutal murderer and would kill without any remorse or thought of what he was ordering or whose lives he was destroying. To Al, it was simply business, and if someone was in the way of his business then that person needed to be dealt with…permanently.

Perhaps the most well-known case of Capone dealing with a rival business problem occurred on February 14, 1929. "Bugs" Moran had been testing Capone for more than a year, but after Moran tried to have Capone's friend Jack McGurn killed, Scarface had had enough. So on that fateful day in 1929, McGurn and Capone lured the rival gangsters to a bootlegger's garage with the promise of buying whiskey. When Moran and his cohorts arrived at the garage, Capone's men, who were dressed in stolen police uniforms, were waiting for them. Thinking that the rival gangsters were real cops, Moran and his men lined up against the back wall for "questioning" and were promptly gunned down in cold blood.

Al Capone went unpunished for the St. Valentine's Day Massacre because of a lack of evidence. Even though the authorities couldn't pin the murders

Al "Scarface" Capone has often been heard playing his banjo in the prison showers. Al was part of the prison band and practiced by himself for his safety.

on Scarface, they knew that he was responsible. More importantly, the public knew it as well. Capone's image was forever destroyed in the eyes of those who once thought of him as the benevolent gangster, and his fame and power began to wane. Capone's end came in 1931 when he was tried and convicted on twenty-two counts of income tax evasion and sentenced to eleven years in a federal penitentiary.

Scarface Capone was sent to Alcatraz prison, where even his fame and fortune did him no good. Al was put into a regular cell in general population. There, he worked as the other inmates worked, ate the same food and adhered to the same schedule. He even joined the prison band. Al Capone was completely miserable the whole time he was incarcerated on the Rock. In 1939, suffering severe brain deterioration from advanced syphilis he had contracted years earlier, Capone was granted early release and spent the remainder of his life in Florida with his mental state that of a child. Capone died in 1947 peacefully at his estate. This was not to be the end of the story for Scarface, however.

Throughout Al Capone's life, he had been bothered by the thought of spirits. Al was never one to be frightened by anything—other than the loss of affection from his "adoring" public—but he had always been terrified of ghosts. One such spirit was the ghost of James "Jimmy" Clark, one of Scarface's victims in the Valentine's Day Massacre.

Jimmy didn't make himself known to Capone until Al was incarcerated in 1929–30 at Philadelphia's Eastern State Penitentiary, where he had been locked up on a concealed weapons charge. Scarface had bribed the warden and guards to allow him special favors such as gourmet food, unlimited visitor rights and luxury appointments set up in his cell. Al Capone's time at Eastern State was more comfortable than most people had it on the outside—that is, except for Jimmy living in the cell with him. Almost every night, the other prisoners would be woken up by the sound of Capone screaming out for Jimmy to leave him alone. This happened so often that the other convicts asked the guards to have Al moved. It got to be so bad that Al could be heard holding whole conversations with Jimmy. Al told anyone who would listen that all he had to do is get out of Eastern State and Jimmy would be out of his life for good. Unfortunately, this was not to be the case. Once Scarface got out of jail, Jimmy followed him wherever he went. It got to be so bad that Capone hired a psychic to talk to Jimmy in the hopes he would go away. No such luck. Jimmy even followed Scarface to Alcatraz and was present at Al's bedside the day he died.

Al Capone likes to travel in the afterlife. He is seen in quite a few places, including a yacht that he once possessed called the *Duchess III*. Al liked to fish from this vessel and seems to still enjoy the pastime. Another place he is frequently reported is the old Eastern State Penitentiary. Even today, Eastern State has a mockup of Al Capone's cell to show just how well he lived prison life there. Not so once he arrived at Alcatraz, however.

When Capone was sentenced to eleven years for tax evasion in 1931, he was sent to a federal prison in Atlanta, Georgia. Afraid that he would be able to re-create his lavish prison lifestyle there, the feds had him transferred to the most secure, most rigid prison in American history: Alcatraz. There, Scarface tried his best to get into the good graces of the warden and guards but failed miserably in all of his attempts. The Rock had beaten him.

Ever since Alcatraz has been open as a tourist attraction, guests and rangers alike have reported hearing the sound of phantom banjo music coming from Capone's old cell. One ranger who was walking the cellblocks before closing one evening said that as he was nearing Capone's cell on B block, he could hear banjo music coming from the tiny cubicle. Thinking that a guest had stayed behind, the ranger hurried to the cell, but once there, the music stopped and he found the cell empty. As soon as the ranger walked away and reached the end of the cellblock, the music again wafted from

Capone has not only been spotted in his cell and the showers but in the laundry distribution area next to the showers as well.

the empty jail cell. This was one of the earliest accounts of Capone's banjo reported within the prison.

It is said that Capone became a loner after he realized he could not bribe the prison officials. Some say he was afraid the other inmates might try to harm or even kill him as a way of gaining notoriety. Because of this, Capone asked if he could practice with his banjo in private while the rest of the prisoners were out in the recreation yard. Even though this was generally not allowed, the warden permitted it due to Al's decline in health. One of the places that Capone would practice was down near the shower facilities. It was usually empty while the other inmates were in the yard, there were guards nearby to keep an eye on and out for him and Capone liked the way the banjo sounded against the acoustics of the large room.

Today, one of the first areas guests tour when they enter the prison proper is the showers. Many times over the years, tourists have come to the rangers and tour guides to ask about the banjo music they hear playing in the shower room. At first, those working on Alcatraz were at a loss to explain the music, but over time, as more employees heard the banjo coming from B133, Capone's old cell, along with the history of

Capone using the shower room to practice for the Rock Islanders, the prison band Al played with, it became clear where the music was coming from: Scarface himself.

No one knows why Al Capone would return to Alcatraz in the afterlife, a place he hated and feared while incarcerated within its walls. Maybe because his mind was already ravaged by the syphilis even before he arrived on the island, his spirit isn't aware that it was a place he dreaded. Maybe the fact that playing music was something he truly enjoyed and he was able to be part of the prison band outweighs his trepidation of prison life and the fear he felt around the other inmates. We may never know. But one thing seems clear: many people feel sure that Al "Scarface" Capone is still an inmate of "Hellcatraz."

CHAPTER 8

GHOST TALES FROM RANGERS, TOUR GUIDES AND GUARDS

From the time this small island came to be known by the native peoples of the area, tales have been told about its eerie spirits. The Ohlone, Spaniards, Mexicans and Americans all have their stories of odd happenings and strange occurrences. For those who have spent long nights guarding prisoners of the island, or keeping the island safe from trespassers, those nights can sometimes be filled with boredom, sometimes with personal thoughts or, on many occasions, with fear and trepidation. Here are just a few of those tales from those who have spent time working on Alcatraz.

EYE SEE YOU

The tales of the red-eyed monster prowling the grounds of Alcatraz are well known, but none of these stories have made their way into the prison itself. That is, until a guard claimed to have seen a red-eyed man watching him in D block.

This story came to us from a ranger who had worked on the island for many years. He claimed to have heard it himself from a visiting ex-inmate while he escorted the man around the island he had spent so much time on.

Back in the late '50s, there was a guard who had a tendency to think of the prisoners as less than men. As such, the guard developed a mean streak toward the inmates that was well out of keeping with accepted norms. One evening while the prisoners were at dinner, one of the inmates got belligerent with another convict and threw his tray at the man. Discipline on Alcatraz was strict, and the inmate who threw the tray was promptly escorted to the "hole" in D block. The guard in question seemed to be in a particularly bad mood that evening and, according to the ex-con telling the story, beat the offending inmate before placing him in the isolation cell.

Later that evening while the guard was making his rounds of D block, he entered the corridor and saw what he thought was the prisoner he had placed in D12 solitary standing at the end of the block near D14. The guard called out to the inmate, telling him to stand still and keep his hands visible, and cautiously approached the convict. The inmate just stood there staring at the approaching guard. As the guard got closer to the waiting convict, he noticed that the man's eyes seemed to be glowing a deep red. It was as if the inmate was staring into a fire and his eyes were reflecting the color of the flames. The inmate still made no attempt to move but continued to gaze at the guard coming closer.

The prison guard slowed his approach and finally stopped about ten feet away from the man he thought was the prisoner he had put into solitary a few hours earlier. Now, as he could clearly make out the face of the man standing before him, he realized that it was someone he didn't recognize. It wasn't an inmate, guard or prison official. As he was about to tell the man to face the wall, the intruder's eyes flashed and a menacing smile crossed his face. The intruder then turned and slowly made his way out of the door he was standing next to and disappeared around the corner.

The guard quickly ran to the door, but just as he was about to go around the corner himself, he felt someone shove him from behind, and he violently crashed to the ground. At the same time he fell, he heard the sound of laughter coming from D block. The guard hurriedly got to his feet, his hands and knees scraped and hurting, and went back to the block to catch the person responsible for pushing him. He found no one and realized the laughter was coming from the cell where he had locked up the unruly prisoner earlier that evening. The guard checked the locks on the cell doors and found them all secure, and no trace of an intruder was ever found.

The ex-con who was telling this tale said that the other prisoners had seen this same man on many occasions. He also said that many of the guards knew about this person but refused to talk about him due to the fact that he was a ghost. The former inmate said that this spirit had attacked others over the years but seemed to concentrate on the guards, especially those with a penchant for derision toward the inmates.

"Well," said the ex-con with a laugh, "I guess that bastard got off easy that night."

WHISPERS IN THE DARK

The Dungeon of Alcatraz is really nothing more than the old basement of the original Citadel. It became known as the Dungeon because of its use as a solitary confinement area for the prison. The guards also decided, for a time, that those prisoners placed there were fair game for torture. Hence, the name began to circulate among not only the inhabitants of the island but in the American populace as well.

While visiting the prison with our group Planet Paranormal, we had given out our business cards to many employees working on Alcatraz, and when one of the tour guides called to see if we were still interested in hearing a story, we jumped at the chance. This gentleman asked us not to think him crazy but said that he had been working one afternoon getting things ready for one of the island's famous "After Dark" tours and was making the rounds trying to clear out the day visitors. He was just about to exit through the door on A block that would take him to the lower level of the cellblock when he heard crying coming from behind him. He said it sounded like a woman, and he was afraid one of the guests—possibly even a child—might have gotten lost from her group.

The guide turned around and followed the sobbing and realized that it was coming from the area below A block that many call the Dungeon. He quickly went over to the locked door and called down asking if someone was there and was shocked when a voice came from below and whispered, "I'm locked in. Can you please help me?"

The guide couldn't figure out how the woman managed to get into the lower section of the prison because that had not been on any of the tour agendas for the day and as such had remained securely locked up. Regardless of how she had gotten down there, he needed to get her out. Unfortunately, he did not have the keys to the lower level and wasn't sure who did. He called down to the woman and said he had to run down to the offices to find the keys and would be back as soon as he could. He said the woman whispered back not to leave her, that she was scared to be down there by herself. He told her he had no choice because he had no way to let her out and again promised to be right back. Then he left to go down and find someone with the keys.

The guide said that he ran into a co-worker near the showers and told them what was going on and to please go find a way to let the poor woman out of the Dungeon while he went back upstairs to try and reassure the lady that everything would be all right. As his colleague left, he hurried back

The Dungeon is nothing more than the old basement of the original Citadel. There are many dead ends, dark passageways and cold, damp alcoves, making it easy to become disoriented and lost.

upstairs. He said he could hear her sobbing again as he entered A block, and he began talking to her before he even got near the door in the floor.

The guide said that the woman whispered up to him again for him to please let her out, that she was scared and didn't know how she had gotten into the basement. He still couldn't see the woman and asked her to come closer so they could talk face to face. He said what the woman told him was that she "couldn't find him." This caught him by surprise considering that they had been talking for a while now and she sounded close enough that she should have been able to spot him easily. When he asked her what she meant, all she whispered was, "I've been here so long. Why can't I go home?"

The tour guide was just about to ask her again what she was talking about when he heard someone coming through the door behind him. He saw that it was his co-worker and one of the park rangers who was holding up a set of keys. The guide told them to hurry, and the ranger quickly unlocked the door in the floor and called down that it was okay to come up. All they heard was a single sob that sounded far away. They called down into the Dungeon a couple of times more without getting an answer and then went into the basement to find the lost woman. The co-worker stayed in A block to see if the woman would come out on her own.

The guide and the ranger looked all over the Dungeon corridors and alcoves but never found anyone. No one ever came up through the tight stairway, and no trace was discovered of anyone having been down there. There were no unlocked doors or entryways that could have allowed the woman to get into the basement, nor had the basement been opened for more than a month. To this day, neither the tour guide nor his co-worker or ranger can explain who the woman was who asked for help from the darkness of the Dungeon.

FRIENDS FOR LIFE

Some of you may have heard the story that former inmate and, before he died, tour guide at Alcatraz Leon "Whitey" Thompson (AZ1465) was fond of telling regarding his beliefs that the prison was indeed haunted. For those who may not be familiar with it, we thought it should be included. Thompson said that during his time as an inmate, he became friends with another prisoner and spent quite a bit of time with the man. When Thompson was released in 1962, he figured he would never see the man again.

When Leon Thompson was released from Alcatraz after serving four years there, it wasn't long before he was sent to San Quentin for parole violation. While there, he began corresponding with a woman named Helen Thompson and married her when he was released in 1975. His love for Helen made up his mind to never commit another crime. It was Helen who convinced Whitey to write about his time on Alcatraz. The book, being self-published, needed exposure, so Helen and Whitey took five hundred copies to Alcatraz and set up a table in the bookstore. They sold all five hundred copies. The book, *Last Train to Alcatraz*, went on to sell over eighty-five thousand copies, and Thompson became a local celebrity. He went on to become a part-time tour guide on the island as a way to help inform people about the history of the prison and to help deter others from making the same mistakes he made in his youth. Helen and Leon were married for thirty years. Leon "Whitey" Thompson died on June 7, 2005, at the age of eighty-two.

One day during his time as a guide at Alcatraz, Thompson was alone in the cell house waiting for tour guests to arrive when he noticed a large, dark figure at the end of the "Michigan Avenue" corridor. The figure was staring at him, and when he saw Thompson looking back, the man walked around the corner and out of sight. Thompson rushed after the figure, but when he rounded the corner, there was nobody there. Thompson said he was sure the person who had been staring at him was his friend from prison. The way the man walked and the feeling the figure gave off left no doubt in Whitey's mind. The only problem was that his friend had died years before.

"I don't care what anybody says," Thompson said afterward. "That was my buddy."

Leon Thompson said that while he had been in prison, he had often felt as if he were being watched by spirits. He even went as far as to say that he believed Alcatraz to be damned.

THE DOORMAN ALWAYS RINGS TWICE

This story by one of the rangers is not an uncommon occurrence on Alcatraz; in fact, many rangers and employees have told different versions of this tale over the many years since Alcatraz was closed as a prison. But, as this is a firsthand account, we thought it should be told.

A ranger told us that he was working late at night, just walking through the prison and making sure all was well before heading to the room set aside for the employees spending the night on the island. He said he would walk all the corridors and all the levels as a way of making sure no one had gotten into an area where they weren't supposed to be. He had just finished with his last corridor, A block, when he heard the distinct sound of a cell door opening. He said it sounded like it was coming from "Broadway," and he hurriedly headed over to see what was going on. When he arrived, he found nothing out of the ordinary—no open cell doors and no one seemed to be in the area.

The ranger started back to the employee area, and as he rounded the corridor away from "Broadway," he again heard the sound of cell doors opening. This time, however, it sounded like someone had activated the switch to operate an entire bank of cell doors. He quickly sprinted back into the corridor but again found all of the cell doors closed. Shaking his head, he decided that he better have a look on all the floors of "Broadway" just in case someone was hiding out on one of the upper levels.

As the ranger made his way up to the second level, he heard the sound of a cell door opening across the corridor. Coming out onto the second-tier

The back-door entrance into the main cellblock off A block.

balcony, he glanced across the way and saw a cell door on the third tier closing. He hurried back down the stairs, crossed the corridor and made his way up to the third level and the cell where he saw the door closing. The cell was locked, and there was no sign of any intruder. Turning to make his way back, he saw a cell door on the second tier across the way closing. Again, he dashed over and up to the second level and again found all the doors shut and locked. As he once more turned to leave, he saw a cell door on the bottom of the cellblock closing. This time, however, he didn't hurry to the cell. The ranger casually walked down the stairs, strolled over to where he saw the cell door move and, without stopping, continued past the cell and made his way to the employee room.

The ranger did say that as he passed the last cell door he had seen closing, he looked over, gave a smile and said out loud, "You got me." He said he knew it had been one of the ghosts of Alcatraz playing a joke on him.

A WARD OF THE RANGERS

The second year Planet Paranormal was lucky enough to spend the night on Alcatraz, the rangers were more apprehensive in allowing us access to the hospital ward than they had been the previous year. One of the reasons for this had to do with a ranger who despised ghost hunters, and the other reason had to do with our safety, both physical and emotional. It seems the other ranger who was with us that night had an experience up in the wards that he would never forget.

The story that this ranger told is of being up in the medical ward doing rounds one day when he heard someone talking in the surgical ward. As the medical floor was closed off to the public, he thought that some tourists had made their way upstairs and were exploring where they shouldn't be. The ranger made his way into the surgical ward but found no one there. He did, however, hear the people talking from the room next door. Figuring he had just misjudged where the folks were, he walked into the adjoining room. He found this room empty as well.

As the ranger walked back out into the hallway, he thought he heard whispering coming from the hydrotherapy room. Instead of going directly into the room, he made his way closer and quietly stood outside listening to the conversation inside the room. He could hear that it was two men talking, and they seemed to be talking about him. He heard one man say, "Why

Planet Paranormal's Ash Blackwell (*left*) and Brian Clune in the surgical room of the medical ward.

the hell is that bastard following us?" and the other respond with, "He's a fucking guard, why do you think?"

By what the men were saying, the ranger figured they were up to no good and quickly entered the room. He found the room empty. As he looked around to see where the men went, he saw, out of the corner of his eye, something heading toward him. He ducked out of the way of a metal tray just as it was about to hit him in the head. As the ranger stood back up, he clearly heard someone say, "Leave us the fuck alone, asshole."

The ranger said that he searched the entire medical ward for intruders but found no sign that anyone had been up there. When he made his way down the stairs and back into the mess hall, the docent who was stationed there so tourists could ask questions waved at him, and the ranger asked the man if he had seen anyone leaving the medical ward. The docent told him the only one he had seen either enter or leave the ward had been the ranger.

The ranger told us it was because of what happened to him that he was apprehensive in allowing us into the medical ward, especially at night. Once we explained our adventures from the year before up in this same area, that seemed to make him relax enough to allow us back up into the medical wards.

SIMPLY A SERPENT

We are putting this tale in the book merely for fun and put very little validity in it. That said, it does seem to have at least some historical background and press.

At least one guard and a few tourists have reported seeing what they believe to be a spiked sea serpent swimming off the shores of Alcatraz. The guard stated that the serpent was brown in color, had spikes running down its neck and spine and was about twenty-five feet long and fifteen inches wide. The guard said he had seen the creature on numerous occasions and that the serpent could reach at least fifteen knots in speed.

Upon learning this story, we decided to look around to see if this was an isolated event seen only by this one individual. We found quite a few tales from many different people.

One tourist claims to have seen a sixty-foot-long serpent partly submerged on a rocky ledge with its entire body exposed and dipping its tail lazily in the water. Others have claimed to have seen this serpent swimming alongside Alcatraz tour boats as they approach the docks of the island, and others have reported seeing them while glancing down at the sparkling water from high up on the island's upper reaches. Whatever one might believe about these fish tales, there are reports that go back as far as the 1800s.

The *Daily Alta California* of October 31, 1875, had a headline that read, "A Veritable Sea-Serpent in San Francisco Bay." The article dealt with a Colonel J.W. Wood having seen a sea serpent not far off the shores of Alcatraz. As recently as 2013, an article from *Mysterious Destinations Magazine* was titled "Where to Seek the Sea Serpent."

Take what you will from this legend, but keep in mind that tales of sea serpents are as old as ancient mariners and as widespread as legends of ghosts.

CHAPTER **9**

GHOST STORIES FROM
INVESTIGATORS AND TOURISTS

CELL 14D ADVENTURES

As mentioned, co-author Bob Davis had a life-changing event occur when he was thirteen years old when a tour guide on Alcatraz invited Bob to enter cell 14D and have the door shut. That was when a terrifying voice made Bob a true believer in the paranormal. Bob is not the only one who has felt the wrath of that same spirit that inhabits cell 14D.

Don Staggs was visiting Alcatraz a decade after Bob had his experience and had the same thing happen to him. Don told us that at the time he went to Alcatraz, the tour guides pretty much let guests go anywhere they wanted, so he and a friend went off looking for the solitary cells. Once they found them, he went into the cell second down from the cage door, and someone closed the door while he was inside. The cell became totally black with no light whatsoever showing in the tiny room. Don went on to tell us that as soon as the door was shut, he felt a hand on his shoulder and a whisper in his ear that said, "You're mine." Don said that he could actually feel the spirit's breath on his skin as the words were spoken.

Don told us that he has never been afraid of ghosts and that he actually found what the spirit said to be amusing. Don began to laugh, which seems to have angered the spirit, because he said that as soon he started laughing, he heard a growl and the ghost left. Don told us that what scared him wasn't the spirit but that he found out about an hour after this happened that the cell doors weren't supposed to be closed because they stick and will lock you inside the cells if you are not careful. Luckily, Don got out of the cell just fine.

ERIN HAYES-POTTER (PARANORMAL HOUSEWIVES)

I have two stories that come from our night on Alcatraz. In July 2009, we were invited by a paranormal team to spend the night on the island and conduct a full paranormal investigation along with a few other investigators.

In the early morning hours of the investigation, my husband, Leif, and I, along with my friend Kris and our friends from Planet Paranormal, were in the infirmary of the prison. We were rather spread out in the X-ray room with Brian Clune in the small room set aside for the X-ray technician while we conducted an EVP (electronic voice phenomenon) session. While we were trying to get any spirits that might have been present to speak with us or to leave us a message, some of us began to smell the distinct odor of cigarette smoke. Not everyone could smell it, but Kris and I could and so could Brian in his own little alcove. The three of us were making comments about the smoke when I heard Brian say, "Shit." Everyone in the room heard him say it, but when we asked him about it, he swore up and down that it wasn't him. We all clearly heard him and know that the voice came from the little window in the small room Brian was standing in. There is no reason Brian would lie about saying the word, so we assume it was a spirit mimicking his voice. Many involved in the paranormal know that this is a tool commonly used by spirits trying to communicate with the living.

The second incident that occurred on Alcatraz happened as Kris, Kristen and I were walking down one of the cellblocks. We were using a Shack Hack, a radio designed to give a constant sweep of the radio dial, and at this point in my career I was very skeptical of these types of devices. As such, I took everything that came from the Shack Hack with a grain of salt. Cellphones have been known to interfere with these devices, so we had left our phones back in the cells we were going to sleep in to make sure that no interference would happen.

My friend Kris was a newbie at this time, and every time the Shack Hack said a word, she would get a little freaked out. So, when the word "demon" came out of the device while we were standing in front of a cell, Kris was

The mess hall has been a hotbed of paranormal activity for those investigators lucky enough to explore Alcatraz at night.

really beside herself. Kristen and I, being experienced investigators, were completely unfazed.

As we walked down the cellblock, the Shack Hack would come up with words, and we began to realize that the words correlated with the cells we were near at the time. We caught the word "jail" as we stood next to another cell, and even though Kristen and I were intrigued by what we were hearing, we both still poo-pooed it as random. We kept walking with the device putting out words, and then the Shack Hack said the word "hole." Kristen and I looked at each other with amazement because the cell we had stopped at was the same cell where inmates had dug a hole in the wall to facilitate their escape. This escape was made famous by the movie *Escape from Alcatraz* with Clint Eastwood. This hole is still in the cell, along with the fake head the prisoners created to fool the guards who walked by into thinking they were sound asleep in their bunks. While Kristen and I thought all of this was rather cool, Kris was beginning to freak out. Kris told us that if the box said the word demon one more time, she was "out of there."

For the next twenty minutes or so, the Shack Hack continued to spit out words that had a direct meaning to whatever cell we happened to be in front of or words associated with Alcatraz itself. Finally, when we had reached the last cells at the end of the block, the device said the words "demon" and "run." These last two words were all that Kris needed, and she bolted out of the cellblock. Having been investigators for a long time, neither Kristen nor I ever run when confronted by the paranormal, but that's not to say we don't get nervous by certain things that can happen when in a haunted location. The fact that almost all of the words that had come from the Shack Hack had been directly confirmed by visual recognition at the time was more than compelling. Kristen and I decided that we needed to go check on Kris due to her lack of experience.

Of Alcatraz, all I can say is that there was enough activity and personal stories we gathered while on the island and enough electronic evidence that we collected that I don't mind putting the label of haunted alongside all of the other descriptors that already belong with the Rock.

JIM VAN EECKHOUTTE (NOPS)

A few years ago, our daughter's Girl Scout troop was holding its bridging ceremony in San Francisco. My wife and I decided to volunteer as chaperones, as this was going to be a large event with numerous troops from all across California participating. We thought this would be a great memory our daughters and I would remember the rest of our lives. The troop decided to make this a three-day outing, and as such, we had a bit of free time between events, so I suggested we take a tour of Alcatraz. Yes, this was a bit of a selfish choice as I wanted to do a bit of ghost hunting. I knew, however, that my family would enjoy the outing.

We arrived on Alcatraz, went through all of the pre-tour stuff, received the recorders that would tell us all about Alcatraz as we walked through the various areas and headed out into the prison. I was so into the history and aura of Alcatraz that I soon realized I had stopped so many times to examine things that I was now completely out of sync with the recording on the recorder and had lagged behind the group; I wasn't sure where they had gone. I looked around and realized that I was in the pass-through corridor where some of the inmates were killed during the Battle of Alcatraz, and I was beginning to feel a wave of sadness come over me. I'm not the type of person to cry or be overcome with emotion—it just doesn't happen to me— but here I was feeling as if it could happen.

I was feeling like crap and in a corridor all by my lonesome when several of the Girl Scouts I was with ran up and asked if they could hang out with me. They knew my hobby was ghost hunting and were hoping I might find something. There I was, standing in the middle of an area where men died, about to have a crying jag and they wanted to hang out with me. NO WAY. I left them in the corridor, and almost the second I left, I began to feel better. By the time I was back at the end of the cellblock, I was completely back to normal.

I don't know if I picked up on some lingering residual emotions left by the men killed during that escape attempt, but the emotions I was feeling were most assuredly strange to me.

THAT GIRL

This next story is one of those that has taken on a will of its own. It cannot be proven, and we did not get it from actual participants, but it has become an Internet sensation, so we figured it at least deserved honorable mention.

Back in 2014, a British couple visiting Alcatraz were enjoying the self-guided tour and snapping pictures of prison life with their telephone. When the woman glanced down at the photo she had just taken, she was surprised to see the image of a woman in the picture of the vacant room she had just photographed. It wasn't just the woman, however; it was that the woman was

The visitors' viewing room. It was through one of these windows that the British woman photographed the spectral woman.

wearing clothes long out of fashion and a hairstyle just as old. The woman who took the picture knew instinctively that what she had just captured was the image of a ghost.

The tourist said from the moment she realized it was a spirit she couldn't stop looking at the picture. Over and over again, her eyes were drawn back to it. She said she became so obsessed with it that Alcatraz itself no longer interested her. She said that the image in the picture is staring right into the camera "with a knowing look."

"I was really skeptical about ghosts before, but I'm a bit more of a believer now. I do think the woman in the photo is a ghost."

To this day, the woman has no logical explanation for the girl in the picture. "I'm baffled by her!" the tourist said.

PLANET PARANORMAL'S FINDINGS

Investigators from Planet Paranormal have had the rare opportunity to spend the night on Alcatraz two years in a row, and what we found on the island prison was some of the most compelling evidence we have ever come across. That first year, we recorded so many spirit voices on our recorders that it seemed the entire prison complex was nothing more than one big ghost party.

One of the first places we investigated was the old sally port (also known as the killing room) at the upper end of the guardhouse complex. This area was directly above the original holding cell for the island dating back to the 1800s. The cell was nothing more than a square cement room, cold and dank, where they kept what they called "incorrigibles"—those men who were deserters, deviants and malcontents. No one is allowed down there now, but the sally port has a hole in the floor that leads directly into the cell below. Trying to investigate while thousands of birds squawk is a challenge, but what we recorded there that night was amazing. While asking questions of whatever spirit might have been present, we heard a clear female voice call out, "What?" It sounded as if this woman was surprised that anyone would be there trying to communicate with her. As we continued with our investigation, we heard this same spirit cry out in a voice filled with astonishment, "Oh my God!" We looked around for a possible mundane reason for this communication—a woman nearby we had missed or one of the female rangers who may have been passing by and talking to a friend—but found no one. Everyone else on the island was far away in the prison building.

This same woman spoke to us a year later when we returned for another full night of investigating. We were busy setting up static cameras and joking around with one another. Brian became the butt of most of these jokes, and at one point the spirit asked, "Who's Brian?" The voice was clear, and it was unmistakably the same spirit from the previous year.

This makeshift cell had been abandoned long before it became common practice to have women on Alcatraz. With this in mind, we began to research who this unknown lady might have been. What we found out dates back to the late 1800s. It seems that an inmate had tuberculosis when he was incarcerated, and in the confined space of the cell, it spread rapidly to the other prisoners. A nurse was sent over from San Francisco to tend to the ill and ended up contracting the disease herself. The nurse died under the quarantine set up, and we believe she is the spirit who was contacting us.

Another spirit we met two years in a row is what we believe is a young boy who spoke to us in the surgery ward up in the restricted medical ward. It was around 3:30 a.m., and the four of us had decided to go to the medical section of the prison. We had been told that this is the most haunted area of the island by the rangers we spoke to, and after this night, we tend to agree with them. We arranged our recorders around the surgery table, and Laurel Blackwell began asking questions. She asked if there was a doctor present, and we heard a very faint "yes" on our recorders. She then asked what that doctor's name was. We heard a very clear, very strong voice say, "I am Jacob." The odd thing about the voice was that it sounded like it came from an adolescent boy. This in itself is not unusual, as the guards and wardens did have family living on the island, but to find the young man in an area that was off-limits to family members was odd.

The following year, we went back into the surgery room and called out to Jacob. We again heard him, but it was almost the same words from the year before. The only difference this time, however, was the spirit's use of "I'm" instead of "I am Jacob." It is quite possible that this could be a residual haunting, but as the island is now closed off to investigators, we may never know.

We also recorded what we believe to be a prisoner who worked in the pharmacy while we were in that room and then someone who was in a great deal of pain while we investigated the hydrotherapy room. When we were conducting an audio session in the hydro room, we heard a spirit

In this sally port, Planet Paranormal received audio of a woman trying to make contact. The grate in the floor leads to the original holding cell.

saying, "It hurts," and something that sounded like your classic rubber bath duck squeaking.

The most disturbing occurrence we had at Alcatraz prison came from the medical isolation wards at the end of the hallway. These three rooms were for those prisoners who were contagious or otherwise sick enough that they needed to be kept away from all but the doctors and nurses who tended to them. The only way into this small section was through a single barred door. When we were there, the room directly in front of us and the one to the left were being used as storage and were all but inaccessible. The room on our right, however, was empty save for a few metal folding chairs. This room also had an outside door that led to a stairway that led to the bottom floor of the prison near one of the guard towers. As we were very high up in the prison, we did not have any desire to go outside.

We each sat down in one of the chairs and began an audio session to see if any spirit was present but with no results. Brian did notice that his batteries had been drained down to almost nothing, which is not unusual in a haunted location. Because we had not received a response to our queries, we decided to try a different location. As we walked out of the solitary door of the ward, Brian said he needed to replace his batteries and began doing so on the bench just outside the door. As we stood there, we began to hear the sound of chairs moving around inside the isolation ward. We hurriedly made our way back inside and found that the chairs we had just been sitting in had completely rearranged themselves. We once more sat down and tried to communicate with the spirit that had moved the chairs, but again there was no response.

We left once again, and as soon as we exited the small barred door, we once more heard the chairs being moved around. One more time we went back into the room, and now we found the chairs that had been previously moved around were now back in the original spots they had been when we first entered the room. We sat down a third time to conduct an audio session, but this time things would turn out much differently than the last two. As we began the session, Bob decided to alter the approach we would take toward the spirit. Bob told the ghost that if it wanted us to leave, all it had to do was tell us and we would gladly get out and not come back. Apparently, the spirit took this to heart, and right after Bob said this, Ash, who was sitting in a chair with his back toward the wall, was shoved three feet backward and crashed into the wall. Ash was a very large man, so the effort required to move both him and the chair with the force necessary to slam him against the wall was significant. At the same

This photo of the medical isolation room was taken the same night that Planet Paranormal investigator Ash Blackwell was violently shoved into a wall by an angry spirit. The chairs in the photo also moved on their own.

time that Ash was being shoved, all four of us clearly heard a guttural voice say, "Get out!" Naturally, we did as the spirit asked. One of the odd things that occurred after this was that Bob had an overwhelming urge to strike out at the rest of us. He said it was like someone had taken over his emotions and had placed an irrational anger within him. Luckily, this feeling passed rather quickly.

Another area that we found to be active during that first trip to the island was the kitchen. This section of the prison is not accessible to guests, so all one can do is view it through the bars while standing in the mess hall. We actually investigated this area twice on our first night, once while a group of us were present and later, after we had left the medical ward. Our first attempt at finding a spirit in the kitchen only netted some minor results: a few strange shadows playing across the back of the kitchen area and the odd figure just off to the side of our vision that

Members of Planet Paranormal witnessed at least one apparition walking back and forth in this area many times, passing both in front of and behind the guard room.

went away when viewed straight on. Most of what we saw could have been easily dismissed. Later that evening, however, things in the kitchen became much more eerie.

Being on Alcatraz, let alone at night, is enough to make any paranormal investigator as excited as a kid at Disneyland, but to actually spend an entire night free to wander the prison and the island at will is a dream come true. As such, we were not about to let a single second go to waste by sleeping. After we had been "asked" to leave the medical isolation cells, we decided to head back to the prison mess hall and kitchen area to see if we could get the shadow that we believed we might have seen earlier that night to show itself now that it was quiet and the crowd had gone to bed.

As soon as we walked up to the bars separating the mess hall, we began hearing noises coming from the bakery. We hurriedly set up our recorders and cameras and started asking whoever might be present if they could show themselves to us. Almost immediately, we began to see what looked like a shadow in the shape of a person looking at us from around a corner in the back of the kitchen. We tried to coax the spirit out into the open, but whoever was there didn't seem interested in our company. The spirit did wander back and forth in the back of the kitchen area, and we saw him pass by at least ten times while we tried to get his attention. At one point as the spirit was darting past, Ash called out to him forcefully, which caused the shadow figure to momentarily stop and turn our way. The spirit only stopped for a moment, hurriedly moved into the bakery and was gone. We didn't see him again that night, nor did we see him the following year on our return. While researching this book, we came across stories about Alvin "Creepy" Karpis haunting the kitchen and bakery; could it have been his spirit that we saw that night?

There have been many tales told by former guards of a phantom lighthouse that will appear out of the fog and an entity they called "The Thing." This entity is said to have glowing red eyes and will menace those it confronts. While exploring Alcatraz, Planet Paranormal decided to investigate the old lighthouse. The structure itself is closed off to the public, but there are open areas in the entryway that lead into the building. It was here we set up our equipment. We stayed near the door of the lighthouse for close to an hour with no result and left rather disappointed. Later that evening, however, Ash and Laurel were coming back from the exercise yard and, while passing by the lighthouse, said they could see glowing red eyes looking at them from one of the openings inside the

Planet Paranormal only managed to investigate inside the morgue for a short time, but the mournful moan we recorded here makes us think at least one person has remained behind.

lighthouse entryway. Could this have been the infamous "Thing" that the former guards had reported?

There is one other place on the Rock that we had activity, albeit light. The old morgue building just outside the side entrance to the prison proper is another place that is off-limits to visitors, but the ranger who was with us that night had allowed us in for brief moments earlier in the day. When it was Planet Paranormal's turn, we made sure to have our recorders running while we looked around this tiny room. When we reviewed our audio, we found that we had captured a long, low moan.

Alcatraz might not like to speak about its paranormal history, but after spending two nights on the island over a two-year period, the one thing we can tell you is that the Rock truly deserves its haunted reputation. Let us all hope that one day they will allow a unified, scientific study regarding the ghosts of Alcatraz.

Opposite: Cell house ghost. *Illustration by Karl Dahmer.*

EPILOGUE

It is up to our readers to decide what to think about the strange things going on in and around Alcatraz Island. For those who have been on the tours and walked through the hallowed halls of the once great prison, it shouldn't be too hard to make up your minds. There is a sad calmness that seems to be ever present in the very walls and steel bars that make up the buildings and a deep despair that hides in the fog-shrouded rocks surrounding the solemn remnants of the once great fortifications. One can imagine the Ohlone trying to eke out a meager existence while hiding out among the outcroppings and small caves that dot the island and sense the lingering fear as they cower from the Spanish missionaries.

Whether you believe in ghosts or you don't, a trip to Alcatraz Island will most assuredly cause you to have second thoughts about the spirit realm. We only hope that this small book will give you some enjoyment and give you pause the next time you hear something go bump in the night.

BIBLIOGRAPHY

Alcatraz History. www.alcatrazhistory.com.

Calisphere: University of California. "Essay: 1768–1820s: Exploration and Colonial California." calisphere.org.

Colored Reflections. "The Muwekma Ohlone Tribe." www.muwekma.org.

History Is a Weapon. "Alcatraz Proclamation and Letter." www. historyisaweapon.com.

Jones, Doug. "Ritual and Religion in the Ohlone Cultural Area of Central California." Master's thesis, San Jose State University, 2015. scholarworks. sjsu.edu.

Library of Congress. California as I Saw It: First-Person Narratives of California's Early Years, 1849 to 1900. "Spanish California." www.loc.gov.

Manger, William. "Battle of Alcatraz: One Inmate's Story of How the Jail Guards Tried to Kill Prisoners." Mirror, January 14, 2015. www.mirror.co.uk.

National Park Service. "Alcatraz Island: Learn About the Park." www.nps.gov.

Quillen, Jim. "My 19 Days in Solitary Confinement on Alcatraz." *The Telegraph*, January 6, 2015. www.telegraph.co.uk.

San Francisco History. "Escapes from Alcatraz." www.sfgenealogy.org.

ABOUT THE AUTHORS

Bob Davis is a commercial real estate investor by day and a paranormal researcher by night. Bob co-owns Planet Paranormal Radio, Planet Paranormal Investigations and Queen Mary Shadows along with Ash Blackwell and Brian Clune. Bob lives in Southern California with his lovely wife, Miyu, and son, Nick. His daughter, Katrina, also a paranormal researcher, is currently living and investigating in Arizona, where Planet Paranormal investigators enjoy investigating new locations.

Davis has been on over thirty-five radio broadcasts nationally and internationally and has been featured in ten books and publications and two documentary films. In addition, he has been published in the *New York Daily News*, *World News*, the *LA Examiner* and the *Paranormal Examiner* and has been seen on such hit television shows as *Ghost Hunters*, *Ghost Adventures*, *My Ghost Story* and *The Dead Files*.

Brian Clune is the co-founder and historian for Planet Paranormal Radio and Planet Paranormal Investigations. He has traveled the entire state of California researching its haunted hot spots and historical locations in an effort to bring knowledge of the paranormal and the wonderful history of the state to those interested in learning.

His interest in history has led him to volunteer aboard the USS *Iowa* and at the Fort MacArthur Military Museum, as well as giving lectures at colleges and universities around the state. He has been involved with numerous TV shows, including *Ghost Adventures*, *My Ghost Story*, *Dead Files* and *Ghost Hunters*, and was the subject in a companion documentary for the movie *Paranormal Asylum*.

His other books include *California's Historic Haunts*, published by Schiffer books, *Haunted Universal Studios* and the highly acclaimed *Ghosts of the Queen Mary*, the latter two both published by The History Press and both with Bob Davis. He is also the author of *Haunted San Pedro* and *Hollywood Obscura*, the spellbinding book dealing with Hollywood's dark and sordid tales of murder and ghosts. He is currently working on books about the ghosts and legends of Calico Ghost Town and the cryptids of California with his son Carmel.

Clune lives in Southern California with his loving wife, Terri, and his three wonderful children and, of course, Wandering Wyatt!

The authors' book Ghosts of the Queen Mary *was featured in the October 2015 edition of* Life *magazine's "World's Most Haunted Places" edition as the subject for the Queen Mary segment.*